D1642572

Barbarians at the Gate

BRYAN BURROUGH
and JOHN HELYAR

Level 6

Retold by Chris Faram
Edited by Jacqueline Kehl
Consultant Editor: David Evans
Series Editors: Andy Hopkins and Jocelyn Potter

Pearson Education Limited
Edinburgh Gate, Harlow,
Essex CM20 2JE, England
and Associated Companies throughout the world.

ISBN 0 582 43258 8

First published by Arrow Books Ltd 1990
This edition first published 2000

Typeset by Ferdinand Pageworks, London
Set in 11/14pt Bembo
Printed in Spain by Mateu Cromo, S. A. Pinto (Madrid)

Published by Pearson Education Limited in association with
Penguin Books Ltd, both companies being subsidiaries of Pearson Plc

For a complete list of the titles available in the Penguin Readers series please write to your local
Pearson Education office or to: Marketing Department, Penguin Longman Publishing,
5 Bentinck Street, London W1M 5RN.

Contents

Introduction

"I realize if we do this I'll have to work extremely hard for a while. I don't mind that," he declared. "But I don't want to change my lifestyle. I've got a great company, a nice life. I don't want to change the way I live."

Ross Johnson was a symbol of the 1980s American business world. In October 1988, he attempted the largest corporate takeover in Wall Street history. *Barbarians at the Gate* is the true story of Ross Johnson, RJR Nabisco—then, one of America's largest industrial companies—and the business world and finance industry in the 1980s. It is a story of greed and competition among ambitious Wall Street businessmen. Who are Johnson's friends? Who are his competitors?

Burrough and Helyar were both journalists for the *Wall Street Journal*. They wrote a series of articles about the takeover attempt. In 1989, they obtained additional information for the book by doing over 100 interviews. They interviewed all the major people—executives, lawyers, bankers, and Wall Street traders—involved in the story, as well as many others.

Bryan Burrough has worked for the *Wall Street Journal* since the early 1980s. He has also written *Vendetta: American Express and the Smearing of Edmond Safra* (1992).

John Helyar has worked for various newspapers including the *Wall Street Journal*, which he left in 1989. He is currently senior editor of *Southpoint* magazine's business section.

Chapter 1　The Board Meeting

For hours, the two men sat on the back porch talking.

Then, as they watched the Florida sun go down over the horizon, they sat for a few moments in silence. Steve Goldstone wasn't pleased about the predictions he had to make, but it was his job. His arguments hadn't yet persuaded his client. He knew he had to try harder.

"You could lose everything," he repeated. "The planes. The Manhattan apartment. The Palm Beach house. Everything."

"That doesn't change the advantages of the transaction. It doesn't change the basic situation," Ross Johnson answered. "I really don't have any choice."

Goldstone tried again. "The minute you do this," he argued, "you'll lose control of your company. I know you think the directors are your friends, but as soon as you start this, they won't be your friends any more. They'll be under the control of Wall Street advisers—people you don't even know."

Nothing the lawyer said seemed to affect Johnson.

Later, as the two men boarded a jet to Atlanta, Goldstone sensed that Johnson had made up his mind. He looked at the president of RJR Nabisco: a man who controlled the futures of 140,000 employees; a man whose products—Oreos, Ritz crackers, Life Savers, Winston, and Salem cigarettes—were in every house in the country.

"*He believes everyone's his best friend,*" Goldstone silently worried. "*And he's going to do it.*"

◆

The Atlanta air was cool that October evening in 1988, when the directors of RJR Nabisco arrived at the Waverly Hotel. They went into the meeting room and waited anxiously for the meeting to begin. It was the night before the company's regular October board meeting. This was usually an informal occasion, but tonight the atmosphere was different. Johnson had called every director and urged him or her to attend the dinner.

Some directors were introduced to Steve Goldstone and were confused. "*What's an outsider doing here?*" they wondered.

Ed Horrigan, head of RJR Nabisco's largest unit, Reynolds Tobacco, was enthusiastic about Johnson's plan. But he was tense. He had known and distrusted these directors for years before Johnson joined the company. He knew Johnson thought the directors were on his side, but he wasn't sure.

A man Horrigan didn't know walked into the room. A few minutes later, he was introduced to the man—a Wall Street lawyer named Peter Atkins. Atkins, Horrigan was told, was there to advise the board of its rights and duties.

"*Oh God . . .,*" Horrigan thought.

◆

After dinner, Ross spoke. He began his speech with a review of his last two years as head of RJR Nabisco: profits were up 50 percent, and sales were up, too. The problem, as they all knew, was the stock. It hadn't gone up in price since the stock-market crash a year ago. Everything they did to raise the price again had been unsuccessful.

"This company is highly undervalued," Johnson continued. We tried to put food and tobacco businesses together, and it hasn't worked. Our food assets are worth about twenty-five times their earnings, but we trade at only nine times the earnings, because people still think of us as a tobacco company. We've studied alternative ways of increasing shareholder values." He paused. "The only way to recognize these values, I believe, is through a leveraged buyout."

The room was silent.

Everyone in the room knew about leveraged buyouts, often called LBOs. In an LBO, a small group of senior executives, with the help of a Wall Street partner, proposes to buy the company from the public shareholders. To do this, they borrow huge sums of money. Everyone knew LBOs meant large cuts in budgets, which suffered to pay off the debt. They also knew that the executives who launched LBOs got rich.

"No one's forcing me to do this," Johnson continued. "But this is the option I think is best for our shareholders." He stopped and looked at each of the directors. "You people will have to decide. If you don't think this is a good idea, I won't do it. There are other things I can do, and I'll do them."

Silence.

"If you do this, somebody else might buy the company for more than you can pay," one man said. "You might not win."

"That's OK," Johnson said. "The company *should* be sold to the highest bidder. That's good for our shareholders, and we have a duty to them."

A woman spoke up. "Other companies complain about declining stock prices. But their managements look to the future. Why is it different here? Is it a problem of declining sales generally in the tobacco industry?"

"I hear a lot of CEOs★ complaining about their undervalued stock," Johnson said. "But the other guys are afraid to do anything about it. This is something you *can* do about it."

Charlie Hugel, who served as RJR Nabisco's chairman, looked around the room. There were no more questions. He suggested Johnson and Goldstone leave so the board could discuss the proposal. "Who else here would be involved in the management group?" he asked.

★ CEO: chief executive officer

Johnson named the group, and Hugel suggested they leave, too. Hugel was uncomfortable. Johnson was his friend, but something was happening that didn't feel right.

Johnson didn't have to wait long before a message came that the board wanted to see him. Taking Goldstone with him, he nervously returned to the boardroom.

"Ross," Hugel said, "it's the agreement of the board that we're prepared to let you go ahead with your plan." They'd realized that if Johnson had started the LBO process, they had no choice; they had to let him continue. It was their duty to allow the shareholders to consider his proposal. "But," Hugel continued, "the trading price has to be higher than the highest price the company's stock has ever traded."

"Fine, I can do that."

"Then the board is prepared for you to proceed," Hugel said. "If you wish to proceed, the board will have to issue a press release tomorrow morning."

"Peter, do you have a copy of it?" Goldstone asked Atkins. "Would you read it?"

The press release was a problem. When the news of the buyout was public, others could make bids before management had a chance to prepare its own bid. But, Johnson and his partners weren't worried. RJR Nabisco was so big that no one in the world seemed likely to top their bid. No one else would get the cooperation he would from the management team.

Johnson wanted to include the price they were considering in the press release. Without that, he feared the stock price would rise out of control and maybe force his group to bid more than it wanted to.

"The price has to be $75 a share in cash," he said. "It'll look bad if we use securities."

That would be a total of $17 billion—the largest corporate takeover in history, three times greater than the largest LBO ever

4

attempted. They hadn't considered bidding much higher; since they didn't anticipate any competition, that didn't seem necessary.

Suddenly, after all the weeks of planning and negotiations, it was real. They were actually going to do it.

"Now we have to find $17 billion," Johnson said.

He thought of the press release. The group had hoped their plan could remain their secret with the board. Now there would be publicity and competing bids.

Chapter 2   The Rise of RJR Nabisco

Until the fall of 1988, Ross Johnson's life was a series of corporate adventures. He was one of a new kind of businessman—"noncompany men" who said their purpose was to serve company investors, not company tradition. They also took care of themselves.

Johnson was the best known of the noncompany men. He did the biggest deals, talked the most, and enjoyed the biggest perks.

Ross Johnson was born in 1931 in Winnipeg, Canada. After graduating from college, he had a series of middle-level jobs— accountant, salesman, marketer—for the next twenty years, and frequently moved from company to company. He was especially creative in managing his expense accounts. He cut back expense budgets of his salesmen, taking a lot of the money for himself and using the additional funds to entertain customers extravagantly. By combining his ability for spending with his talent for making older men feel important, he slowly moved into higher positions.

In the early 1970s, when he was forty years old, Johnson finally entered management. He became president of the Montreal branch of the American food company, Standard

Brands—makers of Chase & Sanborn coffee and other food products. The Canadian branch was a mess. Johnson quickly fired most of the top executives, replacing them with young men who quickly became his friends. He made friends among the top people in society, rich business people as well as politicians. He was confident and developed a routine that he'd follow for fifteen years—staying up late into the night with his friends, talking business, drinking, and smoking.

In 1973, he was promoted to run Standard Brands' international department in New York. His new boss, Henry Weigl, didn't like to spend money and watched the budget closely. Johnson learned to hide his own expenses and expenses for other managers. The senior managers liked him, and he became a favorite of the board, too. They rewarded him by naming him a director in 1974 and promoting him to president a year later. In 1976, he became chief operating officer, which meant he'd be CEO when Weigl retired.

Weigl was angry. He didn't like Johnson and felt he was a threat to his power. After several problems, Johnson called the board's most powerful directors and hinted that he'd resign. They urged him to wait. When Weigl accused him of not following expense account rules, Johnson resigned. Instead of accepting his resignation, the board made him the chief executive.

Johnson had his own rules. His rule of management: "The chief executive can do whatever he wants." He continued his extravagant lifestyle, drinking and talking business late into the night. He doubled the salaries of many executives and increased his own salary from $130,000 to $480,000.

His philosophy: "One of the most important jobs a CEO has is taking care of the directors." He'd always been good with older men; he treated them like kings. He was also good at making bad news seem not so bad.

For four years, Johnson ran the company without many

problems. There were low profits and market disasters. But there was also fun, money, and perks for himself and his friends. Finally, in 1980, there was serious trouble with the expenses of a senior officer. Another officer went to the board, but Johnson managed to explain the situation. Then he fired his accusers.

After five years, Johnson was bored with Standard Brands. In 1981, he was ready for a new adventure when he took a call from Bob Schaeberle, chairman of the huge food company Nabisco— maker of a variety of cookies. Schaeberle told Johnson that someone had suggested the two companies merge. "I think we should talk about it," Schaeberle said. Johnson agreed to meet.

The two executives met and liked each other. Within weeks, they agreed to merge their companies. At the time, the formation of Nabisco Brands, the name of the new company, was a very significant merger. Everyone knew Nabisco, with dominant brands such as Ritz and Oreo, was the more powerful company. And everyone knew who would be in charge.

Although Bob Schaeberle was the chairman and chief executive of Nabisco Brands and Ross Johnson was the president and chief operating officer, it was easy for Johnson to get what he wanted. Before the merger, no one—not even the chief executive—had any perks. Now, with Johnson in charge, the company was paying for his and Schaeberle's club memberships, company cars, and other perks. Salaries also increased.

Slowly, Johnson took over the company. Nabisco executives were replaced by Johnson's people. Within three years, the top executives were almost all Standard Brands men. By 1984, Johnson was making all the business decisions, and Schaeberle gave him the title of chief executive.

After only a decade in New York, Johnson was the CEO of one of America's great food companies. He was a new type of chief executive. He wasn't an old-style team player; he was a man loyal to little except his own wishes.

Now that he'd reached his goal at Nabisco Brands, he seemed to lose interest in running it. He loved going out with famous people and financing golf events. Instead of planning for Nabisco's future, he spent his time enjoying his extravagant lifestyle.

One of Johnson's rules was, "Recognize that success comes from taking advantage of opportunities which cannot be planned." An opportunity like this came to him one spring day in 1985, less than a year after he became Nabisco's chief executive. He took a call from J. Tylee Wilson, chairman and chief executive officer of RJ Reynolds Industries, the huge North Carolina-based tobacco company—makers of Winston, Salem, and Camel cigarettes. Wilson asked if he'd be interested in meeting for lunch.

"Maybe," Wilson said, "we could do some business."

♦

The two chief executives met in Johnson's office the following week, and Wilson explained his plan. Because fewer Americans were smoking, the tobacco business had been declining for a number of years. Wilson needed to acquire another company so Reynolds wouldn't be as dependent on tobacco for its profits. He thought Nabisco was what he needed.

Although both men were the same age, Wilson told Johnson he planned to retire in two or three years and hinted that Johnson would replace him as head of their combined companies. They talked about arrangements and agreed to meet again in several weeks. Both would talk to their boards before then.

After talking to Johnson, Wilson believed his proposal was possible, but his directors didn't like the idea of merging with Nabisco. Some were angry they hadn't been told about his plan before he talked with Johnson. They ordered Wilson not to proceed with his plans.

Wilson, however, remained confident. "This is still going to happen," he assured Horrigan, Reynolds's chief operating officer. "But the next time Ross Johnson isn't going to have so much power. We'll be the acquirer. He'll be the assistant chairman."

A few weeks later, the talks began again. Reynolds agreed to acquire Nabisco for $85 a share, or $4.9 billion. At the time this was the largest merger ever, outside the oil industry.

Johnson bargained hard on other issues. Perks weren't negotiable. He also insisted that he must be named president and chief operating officer, second in charge after Wilson. Because this had been Horrigan's position, Wilson promised Horrigan he would be the assistant chairman and would be part of the new three-man group that would rule the new company. However, when the Reynolds board discussed the details in a telephone conference, Wilson announced that the "office of the chairman" would be Johnson and Wilson.

Horrigan was angry. "We had an agreement that I was in that office," he shouted. He threatened to resign and wouldn't calm down until Wilson agreed to follow their original agreement. Horrigan knew Johnson had seized power at Standard Brands and Nabisco and believed he was trying to get rid of him even before the merger was completed.

"Ty, I wish you a lot of luck," he said. "Ross Johnson will have your job in eighteen months. Just remember that."

"No, he won't," Wilson replied. "We made a deal. He'll get the job when I retire."

The first few weeks after the merger went smoothly. Because Reynolds had acquired Nabisco, people in the town of Winston-Salem were happy about the merger. Johnson bought a house and tried to become part of the community.

Only Horrigan complained about the Nabisco executives' perks. He hated Ross Johnson. "We'll regret the day we merged with that man," he declared to anyone who would listen.

Johnson didn't like Horrigan, either. "I don't like him and I don't trust him," he told friends. "He'll be gone when I'm running this company."

The differences in the two organizations soon became apparent. The Reynolds people weren't comfortable with Nabisco's perks, and the Nabisco people didn't like Wilson's smoking. One Reynolds planner warned Wilson to be careful. "Standard Brands merged with Nabisco, and now there's no Nabisco left," she said.

Johnson tried to work with Tylee Wilson, but it wasn't easy. The two men were complete opposites, and, unlike Bob Schaeberle, Wilson wasn't easy to control. Wilson followed a schedule closely; Johnson was likely to change his schedule any minute. Wilson liked to be alone at weekends; Johnson liked to party with his famous friends. Wilson didn't like Johnson's expense account or the fact that he was always thinking of new ideas.

Soon after the merger, court cases claimed that tobacco companies had caused smokers' deaths. Reynolds's stock, which had been increasing steadily, fell. "You know, Ty, we really ought to be thinking about doing an LBO," Johnson said.

Wilson was especially upset about this idea. He knew all about leveraged buyouts and didn't like them at all. "Ross," he said, "I don't think much of that idea. I know this is a difficult time, but it's only temporary."

Even though their styles were quite different, Wilson and Johnson rarely disagreed on business matters. Wilson was so pleased with Johnson that he encouraged him to get to know the board members. Johnson quickly became friends with Paul Sticht and the other directors.

After a year of working closely with Wilson, Johnson was ready for a change. He telephoned several directors and told them he planned to leave RJR Nabisco. His work was done after successfully merging the two companies. Only one man could be

Johnson was constantly looking for new deals—for change. Since he was always ready to discuss possibilities, many people called him with ideas. Jeffrey Beck, who worked for the investment firm Drexel Burnham Lambert, had suggested a plan to increase the stock price and make some stockholders rich. Johnson was interested; he'd been worried about RJR Nabisco's low stock price. He agreed to let Beck do the work for free. Beck knew that doing this favor would result in more business later.

Johnson let his old friend Andy Sage take care of the details. Sage and his adviser, Frank Benevento, didn't like Beck's plan, so it wasn't used. Beck, however, proposed another idea—split up the company, selling Reynolds to shareholders and allowing management to acquire Nabisco in a leveraged buyout. He believed Nabisco could be acquired in an LBO valued at around $6 billion. Sage and Benevento liked the idea, but Johnson had a different plan. He didn't like corporate debt, the source of money in an LBO. He told them to forget LBOs for now.

◆

Then friends suggested that Johnson meet Henry Kravis, the main partner at Kohlberg Kravis Roberts & Co.* Recently, Kravis had negotiated an LBO for Beatrice, a huge food company. Johnson knew that the CEO, Don Kelly, had become rich after Kohlberg Kravis took the company private, and they made a $3 billion profit. He told Eric Gleacher, merger chief of Morgan Stanley & Co., he could arrange a meeting, but later Johnson changed his mind.

"We're not going to do it," he said. "LBOs aren't good, and we're not interested."

Then another friend, Ira Harris, an investment banker with Lazard Freres in Chicago, arranged for Johnson and Kelly to play

* Co.: a short form of "Company"

golf together. Afterward, Kelly talked about the unbelievable benefits of an LBO. "You'd be doing exactly what you're doing as a CEO, but you'd make a lot more money."

"I'm happy doing what I'm doing," Johnson said, "and money's not a big problem for me. Besides, look at the size of RJR Nabisco."

At $6.2 billion, Beatrice was the largest LBO ever. Recently, RJR Nabisco stock had traded in the low seventies. "If you want to do an LBO, you're talking about $80 or $90 a share," Johnson said. "You're talking about a lot of money." Johnson calculated: $90 for each of RJR Nabisco's 230 million shares came to $20 billion!

"You should meet Henry Kravis," Kelly insisted.

Johnson was curious and agreed. Ten days later, he met Kelly and Kravis in Kravis's apartment. During dinner, Kravis explained how executives could make millions from an LBO. "If you're interested, maybe we could get together," Kravis said.

"Who'd be in charge?" Johnson wondered. "How does it work?"

Kelly explained his wonderful working relationship with Kolberg Kravis, which had majority control of Beatrice stock. Johnson stayed quiet. He wasn't interested in working for anyone except himself. When he left, he felt sure he could never do business with Kravis.

The following Monday morning, Johnson met with Benevento and Sage again to discuss the possibility of an LBO. The basic arrangement was simple and familiar to all three men. A firm, such as Kohlberg Kravis, works with a company's management to buy the company. It uses money raised from banks and the public sale of securities; the debt is paid with cash from the company's operations and, often, by selling parts of the business.

Benevento showed Johnson how a buyout of RJR Nabisco could work, using $90-a-share as a purchase price. To make it work, they would have to sell everything except Reynolds Tobacco. Johnson decided they didn't have enough money. He couldn't be enthusiastic about cutting costs—or his perks.

"I don't like it," he said. "There's just not enough cash to cover it for me to be comfortable." The possibility of personal wealth was strong, but Johnson couldn't risk his extravagant lifestyle just to get more money. Sage agreed.

Johnson turned to Benevento. "Frank, forget about the LBOs. Let's give some business to Drexel for bringing us some of these ideas, but just let's take care of our own business now."

♦

On October 19, 1987, the stock market crashed. Like the rest of the financial world, Johnson was shocked. RJR Nabisco, which had been trading in the mid-sixties, fell into the low forties and stayed there for weeks. The low stock price bothered Johnson for months. Food stocks rose, but RJR Nabisco didn't. Buyers treated his stock like a tobacco stock, even though 60 percent of its sales came from food products. Johnson didn't know what to do.

He was looking for new ideas when Sticht suggested he meet an important stockholder, Clemmie Spangler. Spangler blamed his RJR Nabisco stock losses on Johnson. He'd approached Sticht and asked, "If I could get the funds to take control of the company, would you be interested in helping me put things back the way they were?"

"I don't think that's possible or practical," Sticht had replied. But he'd agreed to meet Spangler in New York and discuss it. They'd met with a group of Citibank executives who were interested in financing an LBO of RJR Nabisco. Sticht had been impressed and agreed to arrange a meeting with Johnson, who would have to be involved.

The three men met in February 1988. Spangler explained his

15

idea: an LBO, at about $70 a share. He mentioned that he and Sticht had met with Citibank and the bank was enthusiastic.

Johnson was shocked. What was Sticht doing? But he hid his feelings. "$70 is OK with me, Paul," he said.

"You'll own 15 percent of the company, with other managers owning another 10 percent," Spangler continued. "Ross, you could be a billionaire."

Johnson returned to Atlanta and wrote, rejecting the idea. Sticht wasn't allowed to attend the two board meetings scheduled before he retired.

Johnson increased his efforts to raise the stock price. He arranged with the directors to buy back more stock. Having fewer shares available to the public should increase the price. Instead, the price immediately fell back into the mid-forties. Johnson had spent more than $1.1 billion buying stock, and its price was lower than ever.

◆

J. Tomilson Hill, merger chief at Shearson Lehman Hutton, believed Johnson was ready to do a deal, and he wanted his business. He called Andy Sage to arrange a meeting.

Steve Waters, Hill's former partner at Shearson, who'd been forced to leave, also wanted Johnson's business. He was now working with Eric Gleacher at Morgan Stanley. "Every two or three years Johnson does something big," Waters told Gleacher. "Something big's going to happen. I can feel it."

Gleacher gave him permission to form a team of investment bankers to present ideas to Johnson.

◆

By late spring of 1988, everybody knew Ross Johnson was ready to do a deal. He was still bothered by the low stock price. Profits were up, sales were up. But that wasn't enough. As he had at

16

Standard Brands and Nabisco, Johnson seemed to be losing interest in operating the company. He was interested in only two things: having fun and increasing stock prices.

As they searched for solutions to Johnson's concerns about the stock, everyone who analyzed the problem mentioned the possibility of a leveraged buyout. Every investment banker urged Johnson to consider it.

"Why would I want to do something like that?" Johnson told them. "I have a great life; I have a company that's great the way it is."

However, one day at an RJR Nabisco golf game in Colorado in August, Johnson and Horrigan were alone in their hotel room. Johnson expressed his concern about the unmoving stock price. Nabisco's assets and earnings were high, but it didn't make a difference. The stock stayed down. "We're still a tobacco company," he told Horrigan.

Harold Henderson, one of Johnson's advisers, walked in. "Ross, the market's never going to give us what it should. This should be a private company."

"Well," Johnson said, "how does it work legally?"

Henderson explained the process. After management proposed a buyout, a special committee of board members was formed to consider it. At some time, they'd have to make the offer public. And when they did, other companies could top it. That was the risk.

"What are the practical realities?" Johnson asked.

"First, could you raise the money necessary to buy RJR Nabisco?" Henderson asked. It would be the largest LBO ever attempted. "How many businesses would have to be sold to pay the debt? If you're interested in an LBO, you'll need help." He mentioned some Wall Street lawyers.

"OK," Johnson said, "maybe we should seriously see what Shearson can do for us."

"*It'll never happen*," Horrigan thought.

Johnson was ambivalent, but the idea of action was exciting. A few days later, he called Andy Sage and asked him to come to Colorado. As they walked around the golf course, Johnson mentioned his latest idea. Sage wasn't sure an LBO was the solution to RJR Nabisco's problems, but he kept quiet. Johnson told him to call Shearson and have them study the possibility.

Later in the week, Johnson called Charlie Hugel. "By the way," he said, "we're having Shearson examine whether an LBO would be possible for us. What do you think?"

"Frankly," Hugel said, "not much. Ross, why do you want to do that?"

"Well, it's hard to be enthusiastic about running the company now," Johnson admitted.

"Ross, you'll probably have to give up some of your perks. Do you really want to do that?" By the time they finished talking, Hugel thought he'd persuaded Johnson not to consider an LBO.

Johnson, however, was still thinking about it the next day when he received news that his son had been seriously injured in a car accident. After a few days, he decided to work harder than ever; he needed something to do so he wouldn't worry about his son all the time. He returned to his office and studied the company accounts to decide whether an LBO was a good idea.

A few days later, he was ready. He knew he could raise enough money for a buyout. He met with Peter Cohen, Tom Hill, and a few others from Shearson. He knew the project they were considering could result in an LBO three times larger than any others in the past.

"Peter, is this something we can do?" Johnson asked. "Will it work? You're talking about a lot of money."

"Yes," Cohen stated confidently. "We can do it."

◆

Jeff Beck knew something was happening. Johnson wouldn't take his phone calls. He thought about an LBO, but dismissed the idea. Johnson had rejected the idea when he'd suggested it earlier. But something had changed. He took his suspicions to Henry Kravis, whose help he'd also tried to get.

"I think it's time to do something about RJR," Beck said. "We should have a meeting and make an offer."

"You're probably right," Kravis said. "Give me your calculations and arrange a meeting."

Beck agreed. "There's a problem, though. You won't give Ross what he wants." Beck knew Johnson wasn't interested in working for someone else. "He'll want control of the board."

"That's true, we won't give him that," Kravis said. "That's a problem."

Chapter 4 Johnson's Plan

Henry Kravis specialized in LBOs, which he'd learned about from his boss, Jerry Kohlberg. Kohlberg had been doing them since 1965 and had developed the process. After working under Kohlberg for three years, Kravis was an LBO expert, too. In 1976, the two men and Kravis's cousin, George Roberts, formed their own buyout group: Kohlberg Kravis Roberts & Co. They took 20 percent of the profits from every deal and charged a 1 percent (later 1.5 percent) management fee.

For six years, they worked quietly without attracting much attention. Then someone noticed a successful deal in which they took a company private for $80 million, using only $1 million of its own money. Suddenly everyone wanted to try an LBO, and business expanded rapidly.

LBOs became even more popular when junk bonds were used. Of the money raised for any LBO, about 60 percent, the secured debt, comes from loans from commercial banks. Only about 10 percent comes from the buyer itself. For years, the remaining 30 percent had come from insurance companies. Then, in the mid-1980s, Drexel Burnham began using high-risk "junk" bonds. Now LBOs could be done quickly, and Kohlberg Kravis and other firms were in demand. The relationship was always the same: buyer seeks target; target seeks LBO; and buyer, target, and LBO firm all profit from the result. The only ones hurt were the company's bondholders, whose bonds lost their value because of the new debt, and employees, who often lost their jobs.

By 1987, a lot of firms were involved in the LBO industry. Deals where Kravis could once have quietly negotiated a buyout agreement became bidding contests, and prices were high. If Kohlberg Kravis wanted to dominate the business, it had to somehow be better than the competition. Kravis and Roberts decided to go after the really big deals—the $5 billion and $10 billion buyouts that few others could attempt. Since their percentage fees remained the same, they could make more money working on $10 billion deals than $100 million deals. And the fees went straight into the partners' personal accounts.

Kravis and Roberts raised money for a new fund that gave them $45 billion in buying power. This was the largest LBO fund in the world. In addition, they received permission from their investors to secretly buy stock in their targets. This action, known as a hostile takeover, would give Kravis a negotiating advantage with chief executives and allow the firm to profit from the increase in a target company's stock after the buyout.

After the October 1987 stock market crash, several new deals failed, and Kravis had financial problems. On October 5, 1988, Kravis met with one of his favorite investment bankers, Steve Waters of Morgan Stanley. "What's happening with RJR?" Kravis asked. "Maybe we should see if Johnson wants to talk."

Waters telephoned Johnson's office later that day to arrange a meeting and talked to Jim Welch. "Ross is busy now," Welch said. "We'll think about it and let you know."

◆

Shearson had suffered in the stock market crash the previous year more than most firms in the security industry. When Ross Johnson began considering an LBO, it looked like the solution to their problems. An $18 billion buyout could solve a lot of problems, and arranging the largest LBO in history would make Shearson one of the top merchant banking firms.

As Peter Cohen was flying back to Atlanta on October 7, 1988, he thought about the fees Shearson could get from an RJR Nabisco LBO. Tom Hill's team had been gathering data for weeks, although Johnson still hadn't indicated whether he'd do an LBO. Cohen was meeting with Ross Johnson the following morning and hoped to find out then.

The following morning the Shearson group and Johnson's group met in Johnson's office. From the beginning, it was obvious this LBO would be different. Hill had made a plan, but Johnson had his own ideas. He wouldn't agree to keeping the process secret until a deal was made; he knew the board didn't like surprises. And he wasn't willing to let Shearson arrange financing or do anything else that would anger directors if they learned about it. On the other hand, Johnson knew that if an LBO was the best approach, he could get the board to agree—but only if it was an idea, not an attack.

Cohen and Hill weren't comfortable with changes to their usual plan, but they had no choice; without Johnson, they had no deal. The worst thing that could happen was that someone might top their bid. But no one was worried about that happening. RJR Nabisco was too big for all except a few firms in the world to think about attacking. Everyone knew that the only person strong enough to give serious competition was

Henry Kravis. Only he had enough power, confidence, and money.

"Henry won't do anything," Johnson said confidently. "I don't think he's interested in tobacco." Andy Sage agreed. Johnson knew Beck and Waters, representing Kravis, had asked about an LBO. He didn't think they were serious, and he purposely didn't mention them to Shearson. In fact, they were all confident that their bid, if they made one, would be unopposed. They felt certain that no one, not even Kravis, would attempt a buyout this size without the help of a management team.

Shearson believed Johnson could manage his board, and Johnson believed Shearson could raise enough money to buy the company. The firm had never attempted anything like it, but Cohen was confident Shearson could do it. Both Hill and Johnson thought a bid around $75 a share was appropriate; it was $4 higher than the stock had ever traded. This would be a total of $17.6 billion. The $15 billion they'd need from commercial banks was more than twice the largest sum ever lent on a takeover.

"It could go higher," Hill warned. The board would try and negotiate a better price, maybe as high as the low $80 range. Johnson got nervous when they talked about paying more than $75. The higher the price, the more the debt would be. The more the debt, the more expenses would have to be cut. And Johnson didn't like cutting his perks.

"I realize if we do this I'll have to work extremely hard for a while. I don't mind that," he declared. "But I don't want to change my lifestyle. I have a great company, a nice life. I don't want to change the way I live."

Cohen and Hill agreed to Johnson's demands. The future of Shearson's LBO business depended on keeping him happy.

The last and most important point of the discussion was a management agreement. This document would define Johnson's relationship to Shearson; it would state how RJR Nabisco would be run, who'd control it, and how the profits would be split. Shearson was amazed when Johnson demanded control of the board and a veto over major decisions, during and after the deal. A veto was his insurance that RJR Nabisco would be run his way, not Shearson's.

In addition, Johnson wanted a larger than usual percentage of the profits. He insisted on 20 percent or more of the stock in a post-LBO RJR Nabisco, compared to 12.5 percent in the Beatrice deal. Hill calculated that 20 percent of the profits could be worth $2.5 billion to Johnson's group in five years.

The matter was discussed again the next day, but they made little progress. They decided to go home, and Sage agreed to discuss it with Hill the following week.

Before returning to New York, the Shearson bankers tried to persuade Johnson to meet with a group of commercial banks to discuss financing. Johnson refused, saying Shearson could approach only two banks and could only find out if there was enough money to do the deal. There'd be plenty of time to negotiate bank agreements later.

On Wednesday, October 12, Cohen met separately with senior representatives from Bankers Trust and Citibank. Both banks were interested. The question was this: Was there enough takeover money in the world to do it? Bankers Trust's head of takeover lending worked out that they could get $15.5 billion— about three-quarters of all the LBO money in the world.

◆

On October 13, Johnson called Hugel in South Korea. "Do you remember the project we were considering?" he asked. "Well, it's beginning to look good. It's something the board has to consider."

Hugel was shocked.

"We're going to do it," Johnson said. "It's important that you come back and be at this meeting."

Then he asked if Hugel would head the independent committee that would consider his offer. Hugel accepted.

When he arrived home from Korea, Hugel called Johnson to discuss who should be on the special committee. As they talked, he realized Johnson had planned more than he'd told him. When they finished, he called Peter Atkins.

◆

Johnson had assured Cohen that negotiating the management agreement wouldn't be difficult. But Andy Sage had his own ideas when he met with Tom Hill at RJR Nabisco's Manhattan offices Thursday morning. If Shearson wanted to do this deal, it would do it by Johnson's rules. Shearson would have only two of the seven board seats; Johnson would have three; and the rest would go to a pair of independent directors. Shearson would loan Johnson's executives the funds to buy their stock. Shearson would even pay Johnson's taxes. And management would get 20 percent of the profits.

"Andy," Hill argued, "we're using our money. We're taking all the risk. Johnson shouldn't get more than 10 percent."

But Sage wouldn't alter his ideas. As negotiations continued, Hill, with Cohen's approval, agreed that Shearson would take just two board seats and pay Johnson's taxes. But they couldn't agree on management's share of the profits. Johnson wasn't worried, though. He knew how much Cohen wanted this deal and doubted Shearson would risk losing it.

"They'll agree," Johnson assured Sage. "If they don't, there's no deal."

◆

On Monday, two days before the board meeting, Johnson began to feel nervous. He began calling directors, urging them to attend

24

Wednesday night's dinner because it was important. When he talked to Hugel, he mentioned there would be a couple of places on the post-LBO board for independent directors.

"It's something I'd like you to consider, Charlie," he said. "We've worked well together, and I'd like to have you on my team. And as a director, you'd be able to get equity."

Hugel didn't know what to say. *Did Johnson realize he was offering a bribe?*

"I can't do that," he said quickly. "I'll be chairman of the special committee."

♦

Johnson was at home Monday night when Andy Sage called. He was upset because Shearson hadn't reached a compromise over the management agreement. Johnson decided to gather his group and call Shearson to settle it immediately. By the time they all arrived at Johnson's house, it was past ten o'clock. He called Cohen at his New York apartment.

"This has to be done now," Johnson said. "If I have this kind of trouble with you now, what'll it be like later?"

Johnson sounded upset. "We'll work something out," Cohen said. He was uncomfortable with the large percentage Johnson was demanding. He knew how much Shearson was giving away, both in control and money. But an agreement had to be reached quickly if they were going to have a deal. Somehow Johnson had to be made happy.

In less than two hours, Cohen agreed to almost all of Johnson's demands. The management agreement gave Johnson's seven-man group 8.5 percent of the equity; if they achieved certain performance targets, this could go up to 18.5 percent. The package's total value could reach $2.5 billion in future years. Johnson's and Horrigan's personal 1 percent each could be worth as much as $100 million each in five years. Johnson also received a veto and control over the board. It was unlike any major LBO agreement ever signed.

For the moment, both sides got what they wanted. Johnson had history's richest management agreement. Cohen kept his business.

◆

On Tuesday, Johnson nervously checked the stock price every hour. The next morning, he invited Goldstone to his house for breakfast. Johnson told him he'd recommend the LBO.

After breakfast, Johnson went to the office. He made sure each man in the group was comfortable with the LBO. Sage was still ambivalent but would support Johnson. The others supported the idea.

Horrigan again reminded Johnson to be cautious about the board. "These men like things the way they are," he said. "They aren't going to like LBOs."

Wednesday morning, Hugel and Atkins flew to Atlanta. After arriving at the hotel, Hugel went to meet with Johnson, as he did before most board meetings. Johnson seemed happy. He obviously hadn't changed his mind.

When Hugel left, Johnson welcomed John Greeniaus, the young Nabisco president from New Jersey. Although few people knew it, Johnson had discussed the possibility of Greeniaus becoming chief executive when he retired in 1990.

"Johnny," Johnson said, greeting him excitedly, "I'm going to do a leveraged buyout!"

Greeniaus was shocked. He understood that Johnson was working with a group of executives. "*But not me*," he realized, "*not me. He's selling Nabisco. I'm out of a job.*"

He sat there, silent, unable to speak. Finally he asked, "Why didn't you have everybody in the management team?"

26

Johnson explained that it was because Nabisco would be sold. "This is a great opportunity, Johnny," he said. "If you don't like the new situation, somebody else will want you. You're young, you have a lot of opportunities. And if you don't like Nabisco's new owner, you can resign and receive three years' pay. Together with your shares of stock, you can get more than $7 million." He paused and then announced, "Johnny, I'm going to make you rich!"

Greeniaus walked out of Johnson's office an hour later, feeling destroyed.

"*I'll have to do something about this*," he thought.

Johnson remained in his office, alone. In two hours, he'd make the biggest speech of his life.

Chapter 5   Reactions to Johnson's Announcement

As he read the morning papers before going to his eight o'clock meeting the next day, Johnson laughed. On the front page of the *Atlanta Constitution*'s business section was the headline: RJR ISN'T LIKELY TO BE INVOLVED IN ANY MERGER.

"Well," Johnson told his wife, "they certainly think they have us figured out." A press release announcing the LBO effort would be out at nine-thirty.

He went to RJR Nabisco's headquarters and met with the committee. Some of the directors were concerned about how the LBO would affect their $50,000-a-year retirement pay. Johnson urged them to discuss this at a future meeting. They agreed, but Johnson felt their displeasure. The directors had a lot of questions about their other perks. "What will happen to them?" they wanted to know.

Angry, Johnson said, "You'll have to wait and see."

When the announcement reached the Dow Jones News Service, there were calls from the media, reporters all over the world, and worried shareholders. The only response given was, "No comment."

Suddenly, RJR Nabisco was the center of the business world. The media were all there. They knew a $17.6 billion LBO would be the largest corporate takeover in history. It was the biggest story of the day.

◆

Henry Kravis was on the phone in his Manhattan office when his secretary put a note in front of him. "RJR is going private at $75 a share."

Kravis almost dropped the phone. For a second, he was speechless. It couldn't be true.

Paul Raether, a partner in his firm, walked in, and Kravis told him the news. Raether paused.

"My God," he said. "*That's too cheap*," he thought.

Kravis began to get angry. "I can't believe this," he said. "We gave them the idea! He wouldn't even meet with us."

◆

Eric Gleacher was in his New York office when he saw the news on his computer screen. He called Steve Waters and demanded that he come down immediately. Both men were shocked as they looked at the screen: "*RJR? A deal? Without Morgan Stanley?*" they asked themselves.

"Look at the price," Gleacher said. At $75, they quickly agreed, Johnson was stealing the company.

The two men knew the questions that had to be answered: Was this a finished deal? Who was advising Johnson? Who was advising the special committee? And, most important, how could Morgan Stanley profit from it?

Before they could do anything, Waters had to run back to his office to answer his ringing phone.

"What's going on?" Paul Raether demanded.

"I don't know, Paul. As soon as we find out, I'll tell you."

The moment Waters put down the receiver, the phone rang again. This time it was Kravis. "What's going on?" he asked.

"Henry, you'll know as soon as we do."

"Who is it? Who's doing the deal?"

"I don't know. We're trying to find out. It could be Shearson."

News of Shearson's involvement crossed Gleacher's computer screen. He called Andy Sage.

"I have to tell you," he said, "I was a little surprised we didn't get a chance to represent the special committee. Did Shearson do something to prevent us from getting hired?"

"No," Sage said. Gleacher asked more questions, but Sage didn't give him much information.

Waters called Dean Posvar, Johnson's planning chief. "We're working on it as fast as we can, and it should be finished by the middle of next week," Posvar told him.

There was a little time, Waters concluded, but not much. Anyone who wanted this company would have to move fast.

♦

Jeff Beck was also shocked by Johnson's announcement.

"*An LBO? Without Drexel? Without me?*" he thought.

He rode downtown in a car with John Hermann, a Shearson banker he knew. Hermann was excited about how good the deal was for Shearson.

"This is going to be the greatest deal ever," he said as Beck stepped out of the car at his Wall Street office.

Beck could hardly control his anger. "I don't think so, John. I don't think so."

Upstairs in his office, Beck took a call from Kravis. "What's going on?" Kravis asked.

"I don't know, Henry. You know we wanted to meet with

them. Let me call and see what I can learn. I'll let you know."

Beck quickly called Johnson in Atlanta but was told he was in a board meeting. Beck was angry. He had to talk to Johnson.

"This is more than urgent," he demanded.

Minutes later, Johnson came to the phone.

"What's going on?" Beck asked, frustrated.

"Well," Johnson said, "we're going to buy the company."

"It's nice to read about it in the paper, Ross. I don't understand you." Beck didn't try to hide his anger.

Johnson was angry, too. "We've already gotten our primary partners for this, Jeff. And that's that."

♦

One of the first calls Kravis took that morning was from Dick Beattie, his chief adviser. "Did you see this?" Beattie asked.

"I certainly did," Kravis said.

"I don't believe it. We have to find out what's going on."

"Dick, I don't understand it. We talked to Ross. Why didn't he ask us? *I* gave him the idea," Kravis said. "Why's he doing this with Shearson? They've never done a deal."

♦

Bob Millard, Shearson's merger chief, hadn't recovered from his initial shock at the announcement when he took a phone call from Peter Cohen. Cohen had spent the morning watching the stock prices. RJR Nabisco's stock was rising rapidly; it would finish the day at $77.25, up more than twenty-one points.

"God, Peter," Millard said. "This is really wonderful." But he was curious why Cohen had made the public announcement before finishing the deal.

"Well," Cohen replied. "It had to be done this way."

"Why are you sure no one else is going to top it?"

"No other company has the power," Cohen said.

30

"What about other financial buyers? What about KKR★?"

"KKR won't do it," Cohen said. "Henry won't give Ross Johnson the deal we gave him."

Millard reminded Cohen that Kravis had recently moved against targets like Texaco on his own. "Just because they don't have management on their side, Peter, doesn't mean they won't bid for it. Why wouldn't they bid for it?"

"Well, because they won't give Johnson the same deal we did," he repeated.

"But if they buy it," Millard said, "Johnson will take whatever deal he's given. You'd better go talk to them."

Cohen didn't seem to be listening.

◆

By Thursday afternoon, Johnson's team realized it might not be good to have an angry Drexel Burnham looking for a way to be part of the deal. Jim Welch called Beck, who was still angry.

"This is crazy, Jim," Beck said. "The price is crazy. What do you guys think you're doing? Why doesn't Johnson team up with Kravis?"

Welch tried to persuade Beck to remain uninvolved. "We want Drexel to approve this deal, to be our friends," he said.

"Well, Jimmy," Beck said, "I can assure you that we'll approve this transaction. But not the way you're thinking."

"Why?"

"We've been trying to get you to do this deal for two and a half years! We're not going to miss being a part of the biggest deal in history."

"Well, would you consider working with us?"

"Jim, we have other obligations."

Welch called Beck twice more, but Beck remained angry

★ KKR: Kohlberg Kravis Roberts

because Johnson had ignored him. As a result, Drexel, the largest firm in the business, was available to be used by a competing bidder.

◆

After a meeting at the law firm Skadden Arps on Thursday afternoon, Kravis pulled Beck into a conference room.

"What's going on with RJR?" he asked.

"I don't know," Beck said. "But you know we have to do this deal. Are we with you?"

"Don't worry about it," Kravis said. "There's going to be a role for you."

The assignment would eventually be worth more than $50 million to Drexel. Even without the money, Beck couldn't help thinking how much fun it would be to beat Ross Johnson.

◆

Bill Strong, an investment banker at Salomon Brothers, was on the phone, staring at the details of Johnson's proposal on his computer screen. Like every other banker on Wall Street, Strong was curious about the possibilities opened by Johnson's proposal. By Thursday evening, he'd reviewed all of RJR Nabisco's annual reports and financial reports. He was sure that at $75 a share, the price was too low. These guys were stealing the company.

Strong was excited. Salomon had had a number of merchant banking disasters, but this deal could change their reputation. And Strong had the ideal partner in mind: Hanson Trust. Using Salomon's financial skills and Hanson's marketing experience, they'd be an unbeatable team.

Friday morning, he presented his idea to John Gutfreund, Salomon's chairman. Gutfreund was interested.

Strong called his contact person at Hanson, explained the situation, and listed RJR Nabisco's attractions: cash from tobacco, well-known food brands, undervalued stock.

"You put in $1.5 billion, we put in $1.5 billion and jointly acquire it," Strong said. "I need a quick response."

The call was returned at two o'clock.

"OK," the Hanson assistant said. "We'll do it."

◆

By Thursday afternoon RJR Nabisco's executive offices were crowded with investment bankers from Shearson, Lazard Freres, and Dillon Read. Hugel met with the Lazard and Dillon bankers and explained the situation. Both banks agreed to represent the committee for a fee of $14 million each. They would review any bid from Johnson and advise the committee whether it was fair to shareholders. If any other bids were made, which was unlikely, they'd review them, too.

Hugel suggested their review could be finished in ten days, which the bankers felt was too short. Speed would benefit Johnson, and they wondered if Hugel was working for him.

◆

Friday afternoon, Tom Hill was at a meeting at Skadden Arps, but he kept thinking about RJR Nabisco. Shearson was watching for any sign of a competing bid. Hill knew every investment banker on Wall Street would be looking for ways to top their $75 price.

One problem was that too many firms were involved. Hill represented Shearson, Jeff Beck headed a Drexel team, and Bruce Wasserstein had brought in Wasserstein Perella. Hill noticed that Beck and Wasserstein kept coming in and out of the conference room. Both men seemed especially busy today. Hill wondered what they were doing. He remembered Beck's earlier comment, "The price is too low. You're going to have competition."

Suddenly he realized what Beck's warning must mean: *Kravis*.

It couldn't be. Henry Kravis wouldn't try something this big without a management team on his side. Besides, Johnson had said repeatedly that Kravis wasn't interested in RJR Nabisco.

Hill had to find out. He excused himself from the meeting and called Kravis.

Kravis's message was brief. "You know, Tom, you've surprised us with this RJR LBO. We're the ones who gave Ross Johnson that idea. We've had an excellent relationship with you, Tom. I'm surprised that in a deal this size there wasn't an opportunity to do something together."

The conversation was over quickly. Hill was shocked. Something had gone wrong. He called Cohen, who didn't seem worried about Kravis's call.

Hill decided they had to meet with Kravis and called him again. Kravis agreed to meet.

Chapter 6   More Plans

At six o'clock Friday evening, Tom Hill and Peter Cohen went to Kohlberg Kravis's offices. On the way into the building, Hill saw Jeff Beck leaving.

"*So Kravis has hired Drexel,*" he thought. The situation was getting worse.

In Kravis's office, the men shook hands. "I thought it would be useful to have this meeting, Henry, because I sensed you're very interested in RJR," Hill said.

"Yes, I do have a very strong interest," Kravis said.

"But this is our deal, Henry," Cohen interrupted.

"You're our competitor now," Kravis said. "I'm surprised you're doing this. We've given you a lot of business. I guess your clients aren't important to you any more."

"Henry, we have to be in this business," Cohen said. "It's our future. This is Shearson's deal. You've said we'd stay out of each other's deals."

"We never agreed on anything like that, Peter. Shearson is a firm we've given business to. This would have been the perfect deal to bring to us," Kravis said. "This deal is so big I can't stay out of it. We have to be included. And we will be. Maybe there's a role for both of us."

"It does make sense for us to do something together, Henry."

Cohen couldn't make a commitment without talking to Johnson, so the meeting ended. "Maybe," Cohen suggested as he got up to leave, "we can talk more next week."

♦

Kravis wasn't going to wait for Peter Cohen.

By Friday evening, he'd organized a team of investment banks to advise and finance a competing offer for RJR Nabisco. At the top of the list was Drexel Burnham, Jeff Beck's employer, but there were rumors that Drexel was having problems. To protect himself, Kravis decided to hire Merrill Lynch as a second fund-raiser. In addition, he'd use Morgan Stanley, the bank of Steve Waters and Eric Gleacher, for advice. It would be the largest team of advisers Kohlberg Kravis had ever used on a deal. However, he also decided to hire Wasserstein Perella. He didn't need their advice, but he wanted them out of the competition.

Next, he began putting together the team of commercial banks he'd need to raise the $10 billion or more of permanent financing. He called Bankers Trust, the New York bank that was the leading source of takeover financing.

"Henry, there's a problem," his long-time banker told him. "I don't have permission to work with you."

Kravis was shocked. Nothing like this had ever happened before. Peter Cohen must have already hired Bankers Trust on an exclusive basis.

"You can't be exclusive with someone else!" Kravis shouted.

All day Saturday, Kravis considered what to do about RJR

Nabisco. The more he thought, the more worried he became. Everything indicated Shearson and Johnson would finish this deal quickly.

On Saturday night, Kravis consulted with Bruce Wasserstein, who was known for his aggressive methods. "The only way to proceed," Wasserstein suggested, "is to make an offer—fast."

A meeting of the entire Kravis team was set for the next day.

Sunday morning Kravis called Mark Solow, who worked for Manufactures Hanover, at his home. "Is Manufactures Hanover working on an exclusive basis for Shearson?" he asked.

"No," Solow said.

"In that case," he told the banker, "Kohlberg Kravis wants to hire Manufactures Hanover on an exclusive basis for a bid on RJR Nabisco."

Solow was surprised. "We've never done that before."

"Well, you're going to do it this time," Kravis said. "We'll make it worthwhile."

Manufactures Hanover was one bank Peter Cohen wouldn't be able to use.

♦

During that weekend, boxes of financial data began arriving at Lazard Freres and Dillon Read. They'd use this information to determine RJR Nabisco's fair price. Saturday, Ira Harris received a number of documents at his Chicago apartment. He was shocked by what he read. The stock was valued at $81 to $96 a share.

Hugel also received a package on Saturday. There was no mention of the sender's name. The package contained an RJR Nabisco planning document dated September 29, three weeks before Johnson addressed the board. Hugel was especially interested in the values given to the company's shares. They ranged from $82 to $111 a share.

Hugel was confused. "*$82?*" he thought. "*If Johnson's own people* *said the company was worth $82 to $111, why was he bidding $75?"*

He was also curious about the source of the document. Someone, probably a high-level RJR Nabisco executive, wanted to destroy Ross Johnson.

♦

On Sunday afternoon, Kravis's team of investment bankers met in Kohlberg Kravis's boardroom at four o'clock. "We understand Shearson is trying to get exclusive commitments from major banks," Kravis told them. "If that's true, we have to do something right away to prevent that from happening."

"We have to do something fast," Gleacher agreed. "We have to shock them."

After a long discussion of their options, they decided on a $90 tender offer. Ross Johnson wouldn't want to match it. But more important, compared to the $75 proposal, a $90 bid would make it appear Johnson was stealing the company. If so, maybe they could create a problem between Johnson and his board.

Kravis turned to the Drexel advisers. "Could enough bonds be sold to buy RJR Nabisco?" he asked.

"We can do it," said Leon Black. "Don't worry."

When the meeting ended, Kravis went to his office and called his partner, George Roberts, in San Francisco. Roberts was surprised by Kravis's suggestion of an immediate tender offer.

Kravis explained, "If we don't do something fast, Johnson may finish this deal within days, if not hours. A tender offer is the only way Kohlberg Kravis can be certain of being able to participate."

The board would have to respond to a tender offer; laws stated that any target of a tender offer must formally reply to the offer within ten days. The board couldn't ignore them. Moreover, it wouldn't be a hostile bid because Johnson had already made a bid. And Kravis wouldn't complete the offer without the approval of RJR Nabisco's board.

It was an enormous decision. This deal was three times larger than anything they'd ever done before. It was also the first time they'd made a bid without the aid of a friendly management team. Roberts and Kravis agreed to think about it until morning.

Kravis was ready to go home around 10:15 when Gleacher and Wasserstein walked into Kravis's office. "We'd like to talk to you about fees," one of them said. They both felt their firms should receive a fee of $50 million each.

"*This is ridiculous,*" Kravis thought. He was going to launch the largest takeover battle in the history of Wall Street, and his advisers were more worried about their compensation than their plan.

"We're not even going to talk about it," he told them.

When Kravis went home, he was pleased with the evening's events. In the morning, he'd talk with Beattie and Roberts, maybe with Peter Cohen.

Then he'd make his final decision.

♦

While Kravis's team was meeting at his office, John Gutfreund, Bill Smith, and another investment banker were having a similar meeting at Gutfreund's apartment. His firm, Salomon Brothers, was among Wall Street's most powerful trading houses. Gutfreund was ready to move Salomon into merchant banking, and RJR Nabisco would give them their reputation.

Bill Strong was nervous. He was asking Gutfreund for a larger commitment than he'd ever made. He explained his plan. Salomon and Hanson would act as partners, splitting stocks, costs, and control fifty-fifty. He proposed that Salomon should quickly and secretly buy a large number of RJR Nabisco shares and then make a takeover bid. He wanted to begin buying on Monday and keep buying until they'd spent $1 billion.

They were all surprised when Gutfreund agreed to the plan.

♦

The management group had taken the weekend off. Johnson hadn't worried about the threat from Kravis. *"Cohen can take care of Kravis. Everything will work out. Anyway, what can Kravis do? He certainly isn't going to bid $18 billion for this company without management on his side,"* he'd thought.

He'd slept late and watched football on TV with John Martin, his assistant president. Then he and Martin had flown to New York. Monday he'd visit his son in the hospital. Tuesday they'd meet with the commercial bankers and begin working on the LBO.

When they arrived at Johnson's New York apartment at eleven o'clock Sunday night, Martin was surprised to find a message from his assistant. He returned the call.

"Henry Kravis is going to make a tender offer in the morning at $90 a share," he was told.

Martin and Johnson looked at each other, amused. "That's crazy," Martin said.

"Who'd pay $90?" Johnson said.

◆

Peter Cohen was reading when he was called and given the news about Kravis's offer.

"That can't be right," he said. "We're supposed to meet with Henry tomorrow. Why would he do something like that without the benefit of another conversation?"

◆

On Monday, the *Wall Street Journal* and the *New York Times* both carried the news about Kohlberg Kravis's $90-a-share tender offer for RJR Nabisco. Dick Beattie was surprised when he picked up the papers. Somewhere there'd been a leak.

Kravis was angry. "It's Beck," he told Beattie.

He was still angry when he arrived at his office. He called

Charles Hugel, Ross Johnson, Jim Robinson, (the chairman and chief executive of American Express), and Ira Harris, who was now working with the special committee, to tell them about his tender offer. Only Harris answered.

"Oh my God!" he said. Any bid that increased the payout to shareholders was certain to be good news to RJR Nabisco's board. "Henry, that's great."

◆

Peter Cohen hadn't read the morning papers yet when Kravis called. "Peter, I'm calling to tell you we're announcing a tender offer at eight o'clock to buy RJR at $90 a share."

Cohen was angry. "You're making a mistake, Henry."

After putting down the phone, Cohen became worried. Something had made Kravis angry. He had to find out what had happened. He called Shearson's top attorney, Jack Nusbaum.

"Why are they doing this? I can't understand it!" Cohen said, his voice getting louder. "He was supposed to call me."

"How can they make a tender offer, Peter?" Nusbaum said. "They don't have any financing. And he wouldn't do a hostile deal."

◆

Ross Johnson was eating breakfast when John Martin ran into the apartment. "The Kravis rumor," he said, "we're hearing it from too many sources. It's true."

"No," Johnson said, "it can't be true. $90 a share! It's crazy!"

"But it's true."

Johnson immediately thought of Cohen's meeting with Kravis. Something must have happened Friday night to make him angry.

◆

"My God, Henry!" Johnson said, when he called Kravis. "I knew you were rich, but I didn't know you were *that* rich!"

"Ross, I wanted to let you know to be polite. We'd like to buy the company. And we'd be happy to talk with you and see if we can work together. We'd love to have you run this company."

"Well, let's see how things work out," Johnson said. "I'll let you know."

Later in the morning, Kravis phoned Jeff Beck about the leak to the papers. "I can't believe you did this to me," he said angrily.

"I didn't do it," Beck said. "Henry, you have to believe me. I didn't do it!"

"These articles make me believe you did," Kravis said. "I don't want anyone I can't trust. I don't want anyone on this team who's only interested in helping themselves. That's it, Jeff. I don't want you at any more meetings."

Beck went crazy. "Henry, it wasn't me," he said. "I didn't do it! You have to believe me! It had to be Wasserstein!"

After several weeks, Kravis decided that the leak had come from Bruce Wasserstein and accepted Beck back into the group. But he realized that he couldn't trust his advisers. For the rest of the RJR Nabisco battle, Kravis, Roberts, and their assistants worked mostly alone.

◆

Following Kravis's announcement, RJR Nabisco's stock went up quickly. Gutfreund was forced to stop Salomon's plan to buy stock. By the afternoon, their bid was finished.

Ross Johnson sat in his apartment, thinking about the morning's events. "As far as I'm concerned," he told John Martin, "this is all over."

Chapter 7   The Competition Increases

Monday morning, Theodore Forstmann, senior partner of Forstmann Little and Co., saw the headline in the *New York Times* financial section: KOHLBERG BID IS SEEN FOR RJR. He read the story with great interest.

"*They're doing it again,*" he thought. $90 a share was a meaningless price; Kravis could bid twice that much if he was using junk bonds. Once again, Henry Kravis was using a small amount of cash and a huge debt to attempt the takeover of a great American company.

Forstmann was angry. He'd been angry for five years. He hated junk bonds, which were used to raise money for takeovers by every major investor and leveraged-buyout firm. Because junk bonds allowed companies to raise money cheaply and easily, using them increased the prices of takeover targets. All that mattered was maintaining a steady flow of transactions that produced a steady flow of fees—management fees for the buyout firms, fees for advice for the investment banks, junk-bond fees for the bond specialists.

Unlike other companies, Ted Forstmann refused to use junk bonds. He'd always relied on his reputation, but now the success of junk bonds was ruining his business. In 1987, after raising a $2.7 billion buyout fund from investors, Forstmann Little failed to propose a single new leveraged buyout.

Forstmann's main rival was Kohlberg Kravis. Kohlberg Kravis Roberts was the only firm whose success was greater than Forstmann Little's. "Kravis can pay these huge amounts because his money isn't real," Forstmann explained to people. "It only exists on paper."

After reading about the story, Ted Forstmann knew what he had to do. Suddenly the Nabisco deal wasn't just a big deal. It had become *the* deal. It would be the end of his five-year effort to show the world the truth about junk bonds and Kohlberg Kravis Roberts. "*This*," Forstmann promised himself, "*will be the deal in which Kravis is revealed for the fraud he is.*"

But first he had to get involved. He knew that Geoff Boisi of Goldman Sachs & Co., one of Wall Street's top deal makers and Forstmann's most trusted investment banker, was putting together a group of clients to make a third bid for RJR Nabisco.

After breakfast, he went to his office and called Jim Robinson at American Express.

"I don't know what's going on," he said. "But you know my reputation."

"I'll have somebody call you," Robinson told him.

Forstmann was satisfied. It was a first step. But there was another emotion he wasn't proud of: Ted Forstmann knew he wanted to hurt Henry Kravis.

"*This is not going to be the next KKR deal*," he promised himself. "*I know Ross Johnson. I know Jim Robinson. Henry Kravis will* not *win this deal.*"

◆

Monday morning, Cohen, Hill, and the other directors gathered at Shearson. They were angry and shocked by Kravis's surprise attack.

Johnson joined them and demanded an explanation. "Something's gone wrong, Peter," he said. "Something must have happened at that meeting on Friday to make him do this. I thought everything was OK. I thought you were going to meet with the guy. What happened?"

Cohen thought he knew the answer: It was Bruce Wasserstein and the other Wall Street advisers. Their stories about Shearson having exclusive deals with the banks must have forced Kravis to make an early bid

Each of Kravis's advisers, Cohen explained—Drexel, Morgan

Stanley, and Wasserstein Perella—had its own reasons for wanting to ruin Shearson's big deal. The junk-bond offering after Johnson's buyout would be the largest in history. It could make Shearson the greatest challenger to Drexel's control of the junk-bond market. Morgan Stanley probably considered Shearson's bid as a challenge to its own growing power in the LBO market. Steve Waters wanted to embarrass Tom Hill, his former partner. And Hill's involvement was a threat to Wasserstein's reputation.

"Our failure's good for everybody," Cohen said.

As Cohen and Hill began to plan their attack, Johnson said, "Well, I guess this is over. This is the end. Who can compete with that kind of offer?"

Steve Goldstone explained to Johnson quietly that his interests and Shearson's weren't the same. If he did things right, he could get a buyout he could accept. He had a number of options, including joining with Kravis.

Goldstone, Johnson, John Martin, and Harold Henderson walked down the street to Goldstone's office. Johnson thought the situation was like a bad dream. The chance of quick riches was gone. "This is over," Johnson said to the others. "If they have the money, it's all over."

Goldstone tried get Johnson to think about the future. If they were going to fight, they'd have to top $90 a share. Running a post-LBO company at $90 a share would be very different from running one bought at $75. The additional debt would require large cuts of the kind Johnson feared: the planes, the Atlanta offices, and more.

"Ross," Goldstone said, "you have to decide whether you're willing to operate this company above $90 a share. If you're willing to do that, then the next decision is Shearson's. Shearson makes the decisions now. It's not your money."

"No," Johnson said, "I'm not going to decide anything until I hear more from Kravis. Cohen will talk to him and find out what happened. Then, and only then, will we decide what to do."

◆

Kravis's group met Monday afternoon. Dick Beattie called his friend Bob Millard, who worked at Shearson and was a good friend of Cohen's.

"Peter thinks he's going to win because he's working with Ross Johnson," Millard said.

"You know that's not true," Beattie replied. "Bob, you have to explain to Peter that the best deal will win. Can't he understand Henry's ready to do this deal without Johnson?"

Both Beattie and Millard realized that the obvious solution was for Kravis and Cohen to get together and divide Johnson's company. A bidding battle could cost the winner billions of dollars and cause bad publicity.

Millard suggested that Beattie talk to Cohen. At four o'clock that afternoon, he phoned Cohen. Cohen was angry because he'd heard Beattie was working with Kravis. He considered Beattie to be *his* adviser.

"This tender offer doesn't mean we can't still work together," Beattie said.

"If Henry Kravis wants to talk, why did he launch the tender offer? He didn't have to do that. Why didn't he call?"

Beattie tried to calm Cohen. "Peter, it appeared best to do it that way. But we should still talk. You should talk to Henry."

"Maybe," Cohen said. Before agreeing, he asked Johnson. When Johnson agreed, a meeting between Cohen and Kravis was set for Tuesday morning.

◆

Peter Cohen and Tom Hill realized that Shearson couldn't fight Kravis alone. They discussed possible partners. Since Kravis had

45

already taken the obvious ones—Merrill Lynch, Drexel, and Morgan—their choices were Salomon Brothers or First Boston. Hill preferred First Boston, but Cohen had a close friend at Salomon Brothers. Friendship was important on Wall Street, and Cohen wouldn't miss a chance to work with his friend.

That afternoon Cohen took a call from his friend Thomas Strauss, president of Salomon Brothers and second in command behind John Gutfreund. They agreed to meet for lunch the next day.

◆

Jim Robinson was alarmed when he read a copy of Johnson's management agreement for the first time Monday afternoon. It was worse than he'd feared: the veto, the amazing total. It not only bothered him, but it would look bad to the public. Seven men sharing up to $2 billion looked extremely greedy.

Changes would have to be made. Now, a lot of the money promised to Johnson would have to be used to make a bid high enough to beat Kravis. As his best friend on Wall Street, Jim Robinson would have to tell Johnson.

"Ross, we have to do things differently now that Kravis has made a bid," Robinson said when the two men met Monday night. "How many people are going to share in the management agreement?" he asked.

"It could be eight, it could be twenty," Johnson said. "I've always thought a lot of employees would share it. I want to get it to as broad a group as possible."

It didn't really matter whether or not the employees would really share in Johnson's riches. The management agreement had to look good. Jim Robinson would make sure it looked good and would be easily accepted by the directors and the public.

◆

Tuesday morning Cohen and Kravis met for breakfast.

"Henry, I said I was going to call you, and I would have called you," Cohen said. "We never intended to keep all the equity in the transaction to ourselves. It's too big. We're looking for a reasonable transaction. If we can do a reasonable transaction that'll help everyone, we should try. Now, why don't we try and do something together?"

"Like what?" Kravis asked.

"A split. Fifty–fifty."

"That's not going to happen," Kravis said. "That's too much." He wouldn't discuss it further. Then he asked about the management agreement. He remembered Jeff Beck's words: "*They want control of the board.*"

Cohen didn't give any specific information, and he purposely didn't mention the veto or the $2 billion management agreement.

"*He feels good,*" Kravis thought. "*He thinks having Ross Johnson on his side will stop us. He'll be surprised.*"

After breakfast, Kravis went to see Beattie and Roberts in their office. They agreed there was no reason for Shearson to be part of this deal. Ross Johnson was an expert in management. Kohlberg Kravis were experts in buyouts. Cohen had a desire for big fees. There had to be a way to get rid of Shearson.

◆

While Cohen and Kravis were meeting, Johnson was making his own plans. Maybe it made sense to try a partnership with Kravis. The only way to find out was to meet with Kravis himself.

At four o'clock that afternoon, Johnson visited Kohlberg Kravis's offices. He, Kravis, and Roberts discussed the possibilities of working together. "I guess the deal we're looking for is a little unusual," Johnson said. He explained that he wanted to keep significant control of his company.

"No," Roberts said. "We're not going to do any deal where management controls it. We'll work with you. But we have no interest in losing control."

"Why not?" Johnson wondered.

"We have the money. We have the investors. That's why we have to control the deal."

"Well, that's interesting," Johnson said. "But frankly, I have more freedom doing what I do right now."

After an hour, Johnson went out to take a phone call. He returned a minute later, apologizing, "I'm late for a meeting with your friend Ted Forstmann."

"*So Forstmann thinks he's going to be involved in this deal*," Kravis thought.

When Johnson left, Kravis and Roberts agreed it was time for them to act.

◆

When Jim Robinson entered his car after a meeting, he was surprised to find a message from Henry Kravis on his car phone. He called Kravis.

"I want to make you an offer," Kravis said.

He explained his proposal: Kohlberg Kravis would acquire RJR Nabisco; Shearson would receive a one-time fee of $125 million from Kohlberg Kravis and an option to buy a 10 percent share of the company. He wanted an answer by midnight.

◆

When Johnson and Hill arrived at Forstmann Little at six thirty, Johnson told Forstmann, "I've just come from talking with Kravis."

Forstmann couldn't hide his anger. He hated Henry Kravis. For half an hour, he talked about the evils of junk bonds, the sins of Henry Kravis, and the way Forstmann Little could rescue Wall Street from them.

Hill left the room to take a call from Cohen, who had also received Kravis's message. "That doesn't sound like my idea of a partnership," Hill said. "It would be the end of our merchant banking business. We can't accept it."

Cohen agreed. It sounded like a bribe to him.

"That was Kravis again. We've received the most insulting offer," Hill said when he returned to the conference room.

Johnson and Hill soon left, leaving Forstmann confused. "*Was Johnson negotiating with Kravis? If so, why was he talking to Forstmann Little?*" he wondered.

When Johnson went back upstairs to his office, Cohen was there, extremely angry about Kravis's offer. He and Robinson were worried about Johnson's meeting with Kravis. Would Johnson stay with Shearson or change to Kravis?

"Ross, if you want to work with Kravis, you can," Robinson told Johnson.

"We won't stop you," Cohen added.

"Calm down," Johnson said. "I have to talk about this with my people first. Then we'll decide what we're going to do."

By night, the RJR Nabisco offices were crowded with teams of people preparing to top Kravis's bid. Johnson gathered his executives in his office and explained Kravis's offer.

"I'm not going to make a decision alone. We're going to vote on it. You're voting about your careers. We can be partners with Henry Kravis, or we can be partners with Jim Robinson." They all knew what working for Kravis would be like. They also knew that if they chose Shearson and lost, they'd all lose their jobs.

Horrigan questioned Johnson closely about what had happened in Kravis's office. "I don't know what you talked about," he said, "but I don't like it."

"I don't understand you," Johnson replied. "I'm making the biggest deal in the world and you're not impressed."

"They're the enemy," Horrigan said. "I don't see how we can

work with them. We win with Shearson or we lose with Shearson."

The others—Henderson, Ed Robinson, and Sage—agreed. "We picked our partners and we'll stay with them."

◆

In the middle of the evening, Ted Forstmann arrived with his brother Nick, his lawyer, and Geoff Boisi of Goldman Sachs. They were taken into a conference room packed with lawyers and investment bankers. Johnson and Cohen were there. Immediately, the Shearson men asked, "How do you fight Henry Kravis?"

As Forstmann finished his usual speech about the evils of junk bonds and hostile tender offers, he noticed that the conference room had emptied. Only three of the original group remained.

"Where did everybody go?" he asked.

Nobody knew. Forstmann wasn't sure what to do, so he waited. Geoff Boisi began to get mad. "Something funny's going on here," he warned.

◆

At 12:15 A.M., Johnson called Kravis at his apartment to tell him his $125 million "bribe" was unsatisfactory. "Henry, I'm disappointed in you. That was a bad offer you made to them. I thought you were going to be fair. That wasn't fair at all. That's not right." He paused and then said, "I'm staying with Shearson. You can't expect me to abandon the people that are my partners."

"I wouldn't expect you to," Kravis said. "Nobody's thinking about splitting you two. That's not what we do."

It was a lie. Rejection of their offer wasn't good. He needed the help of a management team that knew everything about its company. He didn't like to admit it, but he needed Ross Johnson.

Besides, a bidding war could cost the winner billions of dollars.

Kravis and Roberts agreed they needed a new approach. Kravis called Cohen. "Peter, you know we're not trying to split you up. I think we should talk about this. Why don't we meet in the morning?"

"No, if you want to meet, let's meet right now," Cohen said.

Kravis called Beattie and Roberts, and the three men went to meet Cohen and Hill in Johnson's offices. "This is our deal," Cohen said. "We're not going to be in second place to you or anyone else. We have Ross on our side, and that gives us an advantage. We're not taking any bribes. You couldn't pay us twice what you've offered. It's insulting."

George Roberts responded, "Peter, we've come here to talk about this in a businesslike manner. Why don't you give us some ideas how we can work together? We'd like to consider these possibilities."

"Management has made the decision to stay with Shearson Lehman," Tom Hill began. "Without a deal between us, we'll be competing. You don't have management on your side. This is a hostile bid, and your investors will be concerned."

Kravis was extremely angry. "Tom, I'm not going to sit here and listen to you threaten us," he said.

Cohen interrupted, "This is ridiculous. We're here to see how we can work together."

◆

It was past 2 A.M. when a messenger came to Forstmann in the room where he was waiting and took him to see Ross Johnson and Jim Robinson. Robinson spoke first, "Ted, I want you to know what's going on. Our side is meeting with Henry Kravis in another conference room."

Forstmann stared at the wall and said nothing.

Robinson continued, "Teddy, we're doing the best thing, not

the right thing. It's the smart business thing to do. We don't think anything will happen."

Johnson added, "Management's not going to choose these guys."

Forstmann thought, "*Then why are you talking with them?*" He said, "Well, I really don't agree with you. How can you do business with these guys when you have us? Our money costs 9 percent. You don't need junk bonds. You don't need Kravis."

Forstmann left the room, defeated. "Let's get out of here," he said to Goeff Boisi, who was waiting for him.

"Wait, Ted," Boisi said. "If they can't make an agreement with KKR, they're really going to need us. We could demand our own terms."

Forstmann wanted to fight Kravis and show the world the truth about junk bonds. But Johnson didn't seem to be able to tell the difference between right and wrong, between Forstmann Little and Kohlberg Kravis, and that bothered him.

They waited.

The talks in Johnson's office weren't making any progress. "We're not going to do a deal where we give up control. We can't do that. That's not the way it works," Kravis said.

"We're not going to be second to Drexel," Cohen said.

By three o'clock, it was obvious they wouldn't reach an agreement. Kravis and his team left.

Johnson returned to his office and couldn't believe that an agreement hadn't been reached. "We can't do business without them," he told Cohen.

Forstmann got tired of waiting and started to leave. Suddenly he saw Cohen and his group walking toward him. "Hey, partner," Cohen said, "let's talk."

A few minutes later Ross Johnson joined the gathering. Forstmann turned to him. "If you're ambivalent about KKR, you can't work with me." He paused. "Is it over?"

"Yes," Johnson said. "There isn't a deal with those guys. That was something we had to do. It had to be done, and now we're finished. We need your help. We'd like to work with you."

At four o'clock, they shook hands and parted. As they waited for the elevator, Boisi asked Forstmann, "Are you sure you want to do something with these guys?"

"Geoff," Forstmann said, "it's where the management is. It's where we should start. We need to at least try to work with them."

Chapter 8   The Battle Begins

Cohen prepared to battle with Kravis, who was now ahead in the bidding war. Bringing Salomon into the deal as a full partner was his top priority. He asked Johnson for permission.

"What will they bring us?" Johnson asked.

"Three billion dollars in capital," Cohen replied. "Do you have any objections to them joining us?"

"No, not at all," Johnson said. "And you need the money."

◆

Thursday morning Tom Strauss was in John Gutfreund's office at Salomon's when Kravis called Gutfreund. Since Gutfreund was in Spain, Strauss answered.

"Tom, I understand you're thinking about getting into this deal," Kravis began. "We're good friends, and I'd sure like it if you didn't."

Strauss couldn't believe Kravis's request. RJR Nabisco was Salomon's best chance to get into merchant banking. And Kravis had just hired four banks for the deal—and not Salomon. "This seems like a transaction that makes a lot of sense for us, Henry," he said. "But it doesn't prevent us doing something with you."

Kravis was angry when he put down the phone. He'd sent several projects to Salomon in recent years, and Strauss hadn't even called him before entering the battle against him. But he had more important things to worry about. His tender offer would officially begin the next day, Friday.

Soon Cohen and Johnson would make their bid, and he'd have to be ready to bid higher. Before he did, he needed to know a lot more about Johnson's company. And without Johnson on his side, Kravis had a big disadvantage. He needed someone who knew RJR Nabisco. He called Tylee Wilson and arranged a meeting Friday morning.

Friday morning, Hugel read in the *Wall Street Journal* that Kohlberg Kravis had hired Wilson as a special consultant. He called Kravis, who was wondering who'd leaked the news.

"Henry, if you do that, everybody will quit. If you're worried about management, I'll help you find some good people. But you're making a mistake hiring Tylee Wilson."

When Kravis and Roberts met with Wilson later that morning, they found out that his knowledge of the company was too old to be useful. He wanted revenge. The leak, they concluded, had come from Wilson himself. They wouldn't hire him.

◆

Friday morning, Cohen gave Forstmann a document describing his idea of a Shearson-Salomon-Forstmann Little offer. Forstmann looked through it; the words "junk bonds" were on every page. Forstmann was angry. In addition, it was obvious Forstmann Little didn't control the bidding group. He shook his head—no.

"This won't work," he said. In Forstmann Little deals, his firm had majority control.

When Cohen left, Forstmann and Boisi talked and agreed that Forstmann should make their own proposal to Shearson. He went after Cohen and said, "Peter, this is impossible. Let us prepare something and send it to you."

Cohen agreed.

◆

When Gutfreund returned to his New York office, his advisers handed him a copy of Johnson's management agreement. "You're never going to believe this," one of them said.

Gutfreund read it and was surprised. It talked about much more money than Cohen had hinted. If he understood correctly, Johnson's seven-man group would get $1 billion from the LBO, maybe more. When he met with Cohen later, he told him, "We're going to have an enormous amount of difficulty, unless that plan is rewritten and that amount is lower. It's just greedy."

Cohen agreed, although he thought they should wait until they had an idea how high the bidding might go.

Later he telephoned Forstmann with the new capital structure. Salomon and Shearson would each contribute 25 percent of the group's equity. Forstmann Little would contribute 50 percent. Forstmann Little would also have 50 percent control of the company.

Forstmann was genuinely surprised. "That's great," he said.

◆

Saturday morning Forstmann's doubts returned, "I don't know if we can do this," he told an investment banker from Salomon. "You guys are doing this all wrong. All these junk bonds. And what's this deal with Johnson?"

"I don't know," his friend said. "We're not really in control."

"Well, here's the biggest deal of all time. And Kravis is going to take it."

That afternoon he, his brother, and Steve Fraidin, a Forstmann Little lawyer, met with Peter Cohen and John Gutfreund. "I made a mistake," Cohen began, "I was confused last night. Let me give you the correct terms now."

Shearson's proposed capital structure was quite different from the one suggested the night before. Now Forstmann Little would have the lower debt, not the larger one. Forstmann didn't believe Cohen had made a mistake. He listened closely as Cohen explained the details of the management agreement. Each side could veto everything the other sides did. And Johnson and his management team could veto everything.

"*This is crazy*," Forstmann thought.

Fraidin thought Gutfreund and Cohen didn't realize how their arrangement with Johnson would look to outsiders. "By my calculation, this management contract is worth about $2 billion."

"Is that right?" Gutfreund asked.

They added the numbers. If everything worked as planned, the deal would be worth as much as $1.9 billion. "That's certainly a very big profit for management," Fraidin observed. They agreed.

Then Cohen read the fees. Forstmann thought the list would go on forever. When he totaled the numbers, they didn't add up correctly. Shearson proposed raising $19 billion, but it seemed to need only $16.5 billion to buy RJR Nabisco. "We're raising too much money," he said. "Why?"

"Is that right?" John Gutfreund asked.

"*Do these guys know what they're doing?*" Nick Forstmann asked himself.

"We're out of this," Ted Forstmann told his brother and Fraidin when they left.

His only regret was that Kravis would probably win the deal. Then Goeff Boisi called. Three of Goldman Sachs's best clients wanted to make a bid. All he needed was someone interested in buying the tobacco operations, and he wanted Forstmann to be that person. "You don't realize how strong you are," he said. "You don't realize how powerful your money is. If this deal could meet your standards, think of what we could do. These junk-bond guys have been powerful for three or four years. We could change that."

Forstmann couldn't resist the opportunity to go against Kravis and the junk-bond industry. He thought of a picture: "*The junk-bond people are crowded at the city gates. We could stop them. This is where we could stand at the bridge and push the barbarians back. Wouldn't that be great?*"

He'd do it.

"We don't need Cohen," he said. "He doesn't have enough experience. He'll fail. This will be Forstmann against Kravis. The good guys against the junk-bond guys. You know the rules. No junk bonds."

"OK," Boisi said.

"And," Forstmann added, "Forstmann Little must have a veto over what the bidding group does." Boisi agreed to that, too.

◆

Kravis's problem now was that Johnson and Cohen had all the advantages. They knew all about the company's confidential information and its finances. One of the special committee's most important duties was helping Kravis and Roberts learn about RJR Nabisco. Hugel assured them they'd receive the necessary documents so they could analyze them.

Monday morning, October 31, Kravis began interviewing RJR executives. One of the first was John Greeniaus. Kravis was surprised when he remarked, "I'm not part of the Ross Johnson group. I'm not one of these seven guys."

"Watch this guy," Kravis told Paul Raether. "He might be helpful."

Ed Horrigan and a few others refused to be interviewed. Others gave very little information or stated their loyalty to Ross. After two days, Kravis quit interviewing.

"This is useless," he said. "These guys aren't saying anything."

Slowly Johnson's team was getting close to deciding on their bid. There were two ideas: The Salomon team—Gutfreund and Strauss—wanted to bid $92 a share; Goldstone and Hill wanted to bid $100. Goldstone felt the group favored his plan.

Tuesday morning Goldstone took a call from Peter Atkins, the attorney working with Hugel's committee. Atkins wondered when he'd receive their bid. Goldstone told him, "We'd like to negotiate a merger agreement with you. If you're willing to do that, we'll give you a very, very good bid."

"Why don't you just give me the bid now," Atkins said. "The board's very interested in receiving your bid."

"But Peter, it's not that simple," Goldstone responded. "Now we have an opportunity to negotiate with our competitor. If we do, and we're successful, you'll get a much lower bid."

The chances seemed low that Johnson's group could work something out with Kravis. But Atkins didn't know that.

"You've given us something to think about," Atkins said. "We'll discuss it and let you know."

Chapter 9   Negotiations

After the interviews, Kravis was discouraged. Nothing seemed to be going right. In addition to the unsuccessful interviews, his investors were worried that his bid was a hostile bid, and stories in the newspapers were negative. Maybe it was time to start talks with Johnson. Even though he didn't like the idea, Kravis knew it was the right thing to do.

When he looked at his telephone messages, there were several calls from Linda Robinson, Jim Robinson's wife. She had her own public relations company and had been hired by Ross

Johnson immediately after Kravis's LBO announcement. Since then, she'd been trying to get Kravis to work with Johnson.

Kravis decided to call her. She was glad to hear from him. Her philosophy was that they should all be friends with each other, and she thought the whole fight was getting out of control. People had forgotten their real goal, RJR Nabisco. Their disagreements weren't about shareholder values or financial duties. It was a personal competition.

"I know we can reach an agreement," she told Kravis. "We have to get you guys together. Ross is a great guy. I know the two of you would get along great. This is crazy."

Kravis agreed. "All right. Maybe it does make sense."

Linda Robinson was excited and called Johnson Wednesday morning. He liked the idea. He was losing confidence in Shearson.

"Tell Henry it should be Jim Robinson and me—no one else," he told her. "And this has to be totally confidential. No one else—especially Peter Cohen—must know about it."

That afternoon, she saw Kravis at a social event. "I have to arrange a meeting with just you, George, Ross, and Jim," she told him.

"Fine," he said. "But we should take care of some of the issues ahead of time."

"OK," Robinson said. "What are the issues?"

Kravis wanted majority control of the equity and the board, but he agreed when Robinson insisted on splitting both evenly. But on a third issue he refused to compromise: Drexel had to do the bond offerings. It was the only way Kravis could guarantee a deal this size could be completed.

"Linda, listen," he said. "This is very, very important. Drexel is going to have this role. If that's going to be a problem, this deal isn't going to happen."

"You know Salomon is sensitive about Drexel," she said. The

two firms were rivals at the top of the extremely competitive bond-trading business. "But Ross wants to do this deal. He wants to work with whoever's best. It shouldn't be a problem."

Three points, three agreements. Both Kravis and Robinson were encouraged by their rapid progress. When Linda Robinson explained Kravis's requirements to Johnson, he thought they seemed reasonable. A meeting was set for six o'clock that evening at the Plaza Hotel.

"Henry says it has to be absolutely confidential," Linda Robinson told him. "They're not telling their investment bankers. They're not telling anyone."

Johnson nodded. It was the way he wanted it, too. The less the investment bankers knew, the less they could ruin things.

When Linda Robinson left, Johnson called Kravis. "Henry," he said, "let's give this one more try." Johnson and Jim Robinson would represent the management group; Kravis and Roberts would represent their firm.

"All right," Kravis said. "But no one can know. If I hear anything, I'll know it came from your side. Because it's not coming from mine."

Johnson called Jim Robinson. The American Express chief insisted that Cohen be included. Johnson wasn't sure about that, but he had to agree. He called Cohen.

"I've talked with Henry," he said. "He wants to meet. What do you think I should do?"

"Go do it," Cohen said. "It's the right thing to do for you and your people."

Cohen, Robinson, and Johnson arrived at the Plaza at six o'clock. In thirty minutes, they had a plan for an agreement. Control of the RJR Nabisco board would be split fifty-fifty: neither side would have complete control. The stock would be split the same way. Then Kravis mentioned Drexel, insisting that the junk-bond firm must issue the bonds necessary to finance the deal.

"Why Drexel?" Cohen asked.

"Peter," Roberts said, "we're giving $2 billion in equity. We want to be sure the money to finance the deal will be there." Roberts wasn't confident that Salomon, or even Shearson and Salomon combined, could do the job.

Cohen didn't like the idea of selling bonds under Drexel's control. "You know how they are," he said. "When Drexel works with someone to manage a deal, they take everything. They won't give you anything."

"This isn't going to be that way," Roberts assured him. "You'll get half the fees. All right?"

Cohen quit arguing.

The next issue was that Shearson wanted to manage the selling of RJR Nabisco's assets that would be sold. Roberts argued that investment bankers should do that.

"You don't understand," Cohen said. He explained that, when there's a major acquisition, merger advisers are listed in the advertisements in the *Wall Street Journal* and other financial publications. The placement of the company's name is important. Cohen wanted Shearson to be listed on the left, the position of the main bank, because it would be good for their reputation. But if Drexel was in control, Drexel would be listed on the left with Shearson on the right, a less important position. The matter was left unsettled.

In an hour, they were finished. The three major issues had been agreed on. The lawyers could take care of the details later.

Johnson was thrilled. He finally had a deal. It wasn't perfect, but it was better than losing.

◆

Meanwhile, John Gutfreund went to the RJR Nabisco offices and found them empty. Angry, he called Peter Darrow, a Salomon Brothers attorney, and demanded that he come immediately.

61

"I don't know what's happening" Gutfreund said. "There's a meeting at the Plaza Hotel, and I've been excluded. I don't know why. I want you to get into that meeting, *right now*."

When Darrow arrived at the Plaza, Tom Strauss was in the middle of an emotional discussion with Kravis and Roberts.

"This is our capital," Strauss was saying. "We're not prepared to put in these amounts when someone else controls the bond offerings. Why don't you try us?" Salomon hated Drexel and didn't want to lose history's largest bond offering to them. It would be embarrassing to the firm.

Angry, Kravis explained the importance of Drexel issuing the bonds. "They're the best. They're cheap. We can't afford to take any chances. And you guys haven't done this before."

Strauss and Kravis finally agreed to stop the debate. Surely they could reach a compromise later. Besides, there was a more important matter to deal with: the management agreement.

Goldstone took out a copy and held it toward Kravis. We'd like you to sign this," the lawyer said.

Kravis told him to show it to Dick Beattie. Goldstone found the paragraph he wanted and pointed to it. "I want to make sure you see this and understand it," he said.

It was the control paragraph, stating that Johnson would have full control over the deal. Beattie knew that wasn't important. If they made a deal, Kravis was going to be in control.

Beattie took a copy of the agreement and sat down to read it. Goldstone was nervous. "Promise you won't tell anyone about that document," he said.

After a few minutes, Beattie took Kravis and Roberts to another room. "You're not going to believe this," Beattie said. It was unbelievable: the control, Johnson's veto, and the extremely high returns Shearson was promising. "You can't agree to this, Henry," he said.

Kravis was shocked. It was unlike any LBO he'd ever seen.

"This is crazy," he said. "How could Cohen do this?"

"How many people did you say are involved in this?," Beattie asked.

"Only seven, at the moment," Goldstone said, "but Johnson intends that hundreds of employees will also share in the riches."

"Well," said Beattie, "we can't say yes or no until we have some time to look at this thing."

The meeting ended. Goldstone forgot to ask Beattie for the document back, so he kept it.

An hour later, they gathered again at the RJR Nabisco offices. At 3 A.M., an agreement hadn't been reached. "This is crazy," Roberts said to Kravis and Beattie. "We've spent all night arguing who's going to be on the left and right of the advertisement. How are we going to agree on the important issues? How are we going to work with these guys even if we do a deal? All they're interested in is power and position."

"You're absolutely right," Kravis said.

"Let's go home and get some sleep," Roberts said.

Kravis went over to Cohen and told him they should continue after daylight. Johnson had already left. The disagreement between Kravis and Salomon, he was certain, would be solved by daylight. He'd be satisfied with whatever they decided.

◆

Linda Robinson was awakened by a call from Kravis. "What's going on?" she said.

"We just had a meeting. Things went OK, but we couldn't really tell."

"I don't know what happened," she said, "but I'll find out and call you back."

She called the group at RJR Nabisco. Kravis insisted on keeping Drexel in the deal, she was told, and the talks weren't working out. Everyone was blaming Kravis. "*Oh, no*," Robinson thought.

She called Johnson. He was still at home and knew nothing about the situation at his office. "Things sound really bad," Robinson said.

When Johnson finally arrived at his office at ten o'clock, Cohen, Gutfreund, and the rest were angry. He listened to them debate how to deal with Kravis. It didn't make sense to him. All that seemed to matter was who got the most fees.

"This is ridiculous," he shouted. "No one cares about the company. No one cares about the employees. We have a company to operate. I have 140,000 people to worry about. We have to do something!" Then he left them.

As they talked, matters got worse. If Kravis insisted on using Drexel, they agreed, there wouldn't be a joint deal. If there wasn't a joint deal, it was time to bid. It had been ten days since Kravis announced his $90 offer, Gutfreund and Strauss argued. They proposed to make a $92 bid immediately.

Goldstone argued. "This won't scare Henry away," he said. "It'll only make him angry. And we'll lose our advantage with the special committee. It's a wasted bid."

Gutfreund disagreed. "It's not your money," he said. "We know how we're going to proceed."

Extremely angry, Goldstone left. He went to Johnson and told him the bankers were prepared to make a bid. "It's a serious mistake, and it's going to hurt us," Goldstone said. "But I can't stop them. They're completely hostile. They're not listening to me."

Johnson listened but remained unconcerned. This was a negotiation. Sooner or later they'd calm down.

At eleven o'clock, Robinson, Cohen, and Nusbaum were appointed to make the final trip to Kohlberg Kravis.

"We appreciate your negotiating," Robinson said. "Everyone worked hard. We seem to have problems that can't be overcome. We'll have to go our separate ways. In fact, we'll be making an alternative bid. It's going out right now."

"What?" Kravis said, amazed. He thought the two groups were still negotiating. "Why?"

"We may win or we may lose," Robinson said, "but if we lose, it'll be with a structure that's best for our company and our investors."

When Robinson's group left, Kravis and George Roberts were angry. "Ross Johnson didn't even have the courage to tell us that himself," Roberts said. "I'm glad we didn't join with those guys. It wouldn't have worked."

♦

Johnson was also shocked by the management group's bid. Despite Goldstone's warning, he didn't believe anyone would actually make a bid. Not when they almost had a deal with Kravis. And certainly not without his approval.

"What are we going to do?" he shouted at Goldstone when he saw the news on his computer screen. "This is stupid! You're not going to get a merger agreement." He realized he'd lost control of what was happening to him.

Others were shocked, too. After a meeting in Minneapolis, Hill heard the news from Cohen. "I think it's a mistake," Hill told his boss.

Linda Robinson stopped by Kravis's office on her way out of the building. "We have to do something," she said.

"I don't know what we can do," Kravis said. It was over. In the middle of the negotiations, Peter Cohen had quit. "You've made your bid. You're on your own now."

Chapter 10   Problems

Despite the fact that everyone involved agreed it would be renegotiated, the management agreement hadn't changed in two weeks. Friday afternoon, Linda Robinson took a call from a *New York Times* reporter who was preparing a story about the management agreement for Saturday's paper. He obviously knew all the details.

When Peter Cohen heard about the developing *Times* story, he knew where the leak had come from. He immediately called Dick Beattie and demanded to know what had happened.

"I don't know, Peter," Beattie said. "It didn't come from me. Henry gives everything to everybody."

Thursday afternoon, Kravis had had a meeting of his investment bankers, and the agreement had been discussed in detail. He had thought they should know about it. Any of the advisers could have been the source of the leak.

◆

Johnson slept late Saturday morning at his Atlanta home. When he went downstairs, he picked up his *New York Times* and read the business section headline: NABISCO EXECUTIVES TO MAKE HUGE PROFITS IN THEIR BUYOUT. The story suggested the agreement might be worth as much as $2 billion, an amount Johnson considered ridiculous. No one would believe it. Besides, everyone knew the management agreement was being renegotiated.

He called Linda Robinson. She didn't think the story was ridiculous, but she didn't tell Johnson that. She had to make him understand the situation. "It's not a public relations problem you're dealing with," she said. "It's a factual problem. This is going to kill you."

Johnson's phone rang all day. One of the first calls was from Andy Sage, the writer of the management agreement. Sage wasn't concerned about the *Times* story. He was concerned that Shearson wasn't doing its job.

At his Connecticut home, Charlie Hugel was also getting calls.

His were from directors, demanding an explanation from Johnson. They'd look like fools because they didn't know about the agreement. He called Johnson.

"It's ridiculous," Johnson said. "Don't believe it."

Hugel asked for a letter about the details of the management agreement. In his letter, Johnson suggested his group's compensation arrangements were typical of LBOs and that, furthermore, much of the equity would be given to large numbers of employees.

Charlie Hugel read Johnson's letter carefully. In three weeks of conversation with Johnson, it was the first time he'd heard any mention of employees receiving stock. He hadn't even mentioned it the day before, when they'd discussed the *Times* story.

Hugel thought Johnson was lying.

◆

When Gutfreund read the *Times* story, he was surprised. It suggested Salomon had doubts about the management agreement. Gutfreund called Johnson to deny this and to assure him that no Salomon executive had talked to the reporter.

◆

By Friday, Forstmann's bidding group was ready to bid. Saturday he called Jim Robinson in Connecticut. Robinson knew about Forstmann's new group. "Would you still work with us, Ted?" he asked.

Forstmann thought, "*Why couldn't Johnson join the Forstmann group?*" "Absolutely," he said. "No problem at all. We'd have to do it the Forstmann Little way. No junk bonds. But we'd love to have you on our team."

Then he called Johnson; Johnson returned his call Saturday afternoon. They discussed the *Times* story, and Forstmann assured him he didn't know anything about the leak. Then he began talking about his group.

"You know, Ross," he said, "I think we're the best people in the business. We're your kind of people. You know where I get my money. GM, IBM, GE. I don't blame you for working with all these junk-bond guys. But in my deal there's no junk bonds. Jim asked me if we could do this together, and I said yes. If we could work together, it'd be great."

"Teddy, I'll think about it," Johnson said.

He had no intention of joining Forstmann's team. Forstmann, he believed, didn't have a chance of winning.

◆

The RJR Nabisco directors who gathered at Skadden Arps on Monday morning, November 7, were angry. An anti-Johnson feeling was increasing. They didn't like the negative publicity the company was getting. The story of the management agreement had shocked them. Shareholders were complaining. Things were out of control.

The board's bankers had begun working on a restructuring plan of their own. They needed it as an alternative in case Kravis and Johnson teamed up.

Peter Atkins had written a set of rules telling each of the three groups—Johnson, Kravis, and Forstmann—how to make its bid. Each agreed quickly. The deadline was five o'clock Friday, November 18, eleven days away.

Johnson wasn't happy. A formal auction made all bidders equal. He'd lost his advantage.

◆

Kravis was still searching for someone to help him get information about RJR Nabisco. With only eleven days until bids were due, he was getting desperate. He called Paul Sticht,

and the two men met Monday afternoon at four o'c
obviously cared about the company, but his knowledg
company wasn't current. Kravis, however, realized he didn't
anyone else to help him. The two men shook hands, and Pa
Sticht joined the Kohlberg Kravis team.

◆

Johnson was worried. Nothing about his "Great Adventure" had
gone as planned. And more and more often, Shearson was
controlling what happened. Nothing about this fight was fun.
Most of all, the bidding level bothered him. Even if they won, his
perks would be greatly reduced.

"We can't quit now," Ed Horrigan told Johnson: "If we have to
lose, I want it to be in a good battle, not because we quit. You
have to win, Ross."

"You don't understand," Johnson said. "We don't have to win,
Ed. You can't put your pride first."

On Thursday, November 10, Johnson left New York for the
weekend. That weekend he took a call from Hugel. Hugel had
learned that Johnson had raised Andy Sage's salary from $250,000
a year to $500,000. He was angry; he was certain the board had
never approved the raise.

"The board approved that in July," Johnson said. Hugel
checked the notes of the July meeting and didn't find anything
about it.

For the second time that week, he thought Johnson had lied.

Chapter 11   The Deadline Approaches

"I'm going to make you rich, Johnny!"

John Greeniaus still remembered Johnson's words clearly. "*How
could Johnson do this,*" he wondered, "*and think that money would*

69

make it better?" Greeniaus wasn't interested in money; he wanted Nabisco to be a well-run company. He hated the idea of this LBO, but he hated equally the fact that he hadn't been invited to join the management group. He was angry.

A few days after the LBO was announced, he'd mailed a confidential planning document to Charlie Hugel. It was the first part of his plan. He'd help the directors understand what Johnson was really like, and he'd aid the enemy.

He talked to Nabisco's chief financial officer. "We're going to restructure Nabisco," Greeniaus said. "We'll show how money can be saved and cash flow reduced. If other bidders realize Nabisco's possibilities, they might bid more than Johnson."

He took his idea to Josh Gotbaum, who was on the special committee. "We'll only give this information to the special committee," Greeniaus said. "Ross—and management—can't know we're talking to you. We could lose our jobs."

Greeniaus was scheduled to address the special committee on Monday, November 14. Johnson was scheduled that day, too.

On the twenty-seventh day of the LBO crisis, Johnson met with the board. When they asked Johnson about the merger agreement, he said the *Times* had reported it wrong; his share of the profits was the same as in other LBOs. When they asked for ways to cut costs in the tobacco business, both Johnson and Horrigan said there weren't any. Their attitude was almost hostile.

◆

Kravis needed information about RJR Nabisco. Accurate projections of profits, sales, and cash flow are necessary in order to make a successful bid. And making the right bid is extremely important. The higher the price, the higher the debt. And too much debt could ruin a company.

He'd hoped to learn about profits, sales, and cash flow during his interviews with the RJR Nabisco executives. However, since they hadn't cooperated, he hadn't learned much. By Monday, four days before bids were due, Kravis knew a little about Nabisco and almost nothing about Horrigan's tobacco business.

Scott Stuart was a Kohlberg Kravis partner, and it was his job to develop the projections. This was difficult, since some of the relevant information was missing. In addition, Stuart didn't completely understand the numbers he had. The projections they'd obtained from RJR Nabisco had a heading "Other Uses of Cash." Beside it were amounts from $300 million to $500 million. Stuart didn't know what the heading meant. No one at the special committee knew what it meant, either. He had four days to solve this mystery.

Monday morning, Stuart took a call from a Dillon Read partner who suggested he talk with John Greeniaus. They arranged for Greeniaus to meet with Paul Raether that afternoon. Before they began, Greeniaus asked if Kravis's group was negotiating with Johnson or the management group.

"No," Raether said.

"Good," Greeniaus said. "I have a few things I'd like to tell you." He talked for two and a half hours, telling them Nabisco's operating secrets, its weaknesses and mistakes.

"Nobody's ever asked us how we'd run this business for cash," he said. "There are a lot of things that can be done. Nabisco can increase its operating income 40 percent in a single year if necessary. Cash flow can be increased from $816 million to $1.1 billion.

Raether didn't believe him.

"You don't understand," Greeniaus said. "I'm supposed to produce 12 percent earnings every quarter. The biggest problem I'll have next quarter is getting rid of all the additional cash these businesses bring in. The earnings are going to be too big. I have to spend them to keep them down. Wall Street likes things to be predictable."

"What are you going to spend the money on?" Raether asked.

"Product promotion, marketing."

"Is that a good way to spend it?"

Greeniaus laughed. "No, not really. All this money isn't needed," he emphasized. Then he mentioned some of Johnson's extravagant expenses.

Before he left, Raether told Greeniaus to be prepared to produce the amounts of money he was talking about. If Kravis won, Nabisco wouldn't be sold. Greeniaus was happy.

By the next day, Kohlberg Kravis understood the importance of Greeniaus's information. They could increase their bid from the low nineties to nearly $100 a share.

◆

Ted Forstmann was frustrated. He was comfortable bidding $85 a share and could do the deal at $90. But there was only one way to increase the returns enough to bid higher—junk bonds. Discussions with Geoff Boisi always returned to junk bonds. They argued and argued.

"I guess we should just end this," Ted Forstmann said to his brother.

The next morning, Forstmann Little & Co. withdrew from the bidding.

◆

On Monday morning—before Forstmann's announcement—Peter Atkins met with the special committee. The three investor groups were moving quickly toward the Friday deadline. He was confident their bids would satisfy both the board and its increasingly unhappy shareholders. Everything seemed under control when a letter was carried into the room and placed in from of him. A new group wanted to be involved.

◆

72

When he had seen the news of Ross Johnson's $75-a-share proposal on his computer screen, James Maher, First Boston's merger chief, had immediately called a meeting to plan their attack. Like every other investment banker on Wall Street, they wanted to be involved in the deal. But they'd been left out.

He'd tried everything he could to get involved and hadn't succeeded. Maher was scared. First Boston had been losing business since Bruce Wasserstein had left and taken many of their clients. He was desperate when investment banker Brian Finn came into his office with an idea. He'd found an unusual tax law that would enable them to save as much as $4 billion on taxes by delaying payment on the borrowed money.

On November 9, nine days before the bids were due, banker Leon Kalvaria decided to look over First Boston's list of possible partners again and found a name he hadn't contacted before: Jay Pritzker, a Chicago investor. Kalvaria called Pritzker's adviser, Jerry Seslowe, chief executive of Resource Holdings, who recommended investment options to rich investors.

Kalvaria explained Finn's idea and then said, "Jerry, we have an advantage. We have a tax structure that could give shareholders eight to ten dollars in additional cash, which KKR and Shearson can't do."

The next day Seslowe called Jay Pritzker and persuaded him to be First Boston's partner for the deal.

Tuesday morning, three days before the Friday bid deadline, Finn met with the special committee. He described their plan as a restructuring, not an acquisition. They were offering to work with the board to sell the food businesses, give the proceeds to the shareholders, and leave the tobacco business as it was. They thought this plan would be more acceptable than those offered by Kravis or Cohen. However, the board thought it was too risky.

On Wednesday, Maher received a letter from Peter Atkins. The board wasn't going to allow First Boston to interview the executives. If First Boston wanted to bid, it would have to get information on its own. It didn't seem fair. The bidding deadline was in two days.

News of First Boston's unusual proposal was in the papers Thursday morning. No one seemed to take it seriously.

◆

As the deadline approached, Johnson began to worry about the effect the bad publicity about his management agreement was having on the board. Wednesday he called Hugel and the directors. "I don't think I've done anything wrong," he told each director. "Whatever happens, the management group has raised the stock price, and that's what's important."

That day, November 16, a new management agreement was approved in a meeting in Peter Cohen's office. Johnson had agreed to cut his group's profit to 6.5 percent. It looked like he'd reduced his share of the money, but he hadn't. Johnson and Horrigan had each planned to take 1 percent of the equity for themselves. Goldstone valued that at between $75 million and $100 million over five to seven years. And Johnson still planned to take 1 percent in the new agreement.

◆

The Kravis group's excited reaction to John Greeniaus's information didn't last long. Wednesday night, they realized Scott Stuart had overestimated RJR Nabisco's available cash by $450 million.

"*How good are the rest of our projections?*" Kravis wondered when he heard the news Thursday morning. "*What else don't we know?*"

"How much do we really know about this company?" George Roberts asked on Friday morning when the Kravis group gathered in his office.

74

"Do we really want to do this ourselves?" Paul Raether asked.

They discussed their bid for hours. Kravis and Raether were comfortable with $97 to $98. Roberts wasn't comfortable with anything above $93.

◆

Selecting lawyers to prepare its bid, normally an easy task, was a problem for First Boston. On Thursday, Maher finally selected a little-known law firm. Their first task was to write the formal bid letter that would be sent Friday afternoon. Friday morning they arrived with a proposal. It was unacceptable.

They worked on the letter and debated their proposal all day. As the deadline approached, Maher and the lawyers were still arguing whether to bid for the entire RJR Nabisco company or only the tobacco operation. A few minutes before five o'clock, Maher called Atkins and said their letter might be a little late.

◆

Johnson, Horrigan, and Sage walked into Cohen's office Friday morning. "OK, guys," Cohen said. "What's the price going to be?"

"A lot," answered Johnson, smiling.

They went to the dining room for lunch. Three hours later they still hadn't begun talking about their bid.

"Where's the bid?" Gar Bason of Davis Polk, asked Goldstone at two o'clock. "We're running out of time. If they don't decide soon, we'll have no bid at all."

Bason got the bid just after three o'clock and began preparing the fat bid package that would include their proposal and bid. At 3:45, he and several other lawyers got in a taxi for the ride across New York to deliver it. Several documents were incomplete, and they worked on them in the taxi. Traffic was heavy, and progress was slow.

Two blocks away from the building, traffic stopped. The four attorneys got out and ran to the building. They pushed their way through the photographers and reporters and ran inside. Finally, they reached the office and handed Peter Atkins the package of documents containing the group's bid.

One of the lawyers looked at his watch. It was 5:01. The largest takeover bid in corporate history was late. He hoped no one noticed.

Casey Cogut had arrived with the Kohlberg Kravis bid and walked unnoticed past the photographers at ten minutes before five.

At seven o'clock, two hours after the deadline had passed, First Boston still had no bid. At nine o'clock, Maher ordered the letter sent. There were no television cameras and reporters when Brian Finn and Scott Lindsay walked into the building at nine thirty. Atkins was in a meeting. Finn handed the letter to his secretary, and the two men left.

Chapter 12   The Bids

At Skadden Arps, there was a feeling of relief when the lawyers finally looked at the first two bids. It wasn't even close: Kravis had bid $94 a share, or $21.62 billion. Johnson had bid $100 a share, or $23 billion. "*This is going to be easy*," they thought.

♦

At nine o'clock, Atkins dismissed the investment bankers and directors who'd been waiting. The committee would meet on Sunday morning to formally declare Johnson the winner. When First Boston's proposal was finally passed to him, Atkins read it carefully. It was only an idea. It had no financing. But First Boston was suggesting it could get between $105 and $118 a share. If Maher could do what he said, First Boston's approach could be worth $3 billion more than the other proposals. Skadden's tax advisers would have to look at this.

The lawyers read Maher's nine-page proposal while they ate dinner. At eleven o'clock, Matt Rosen, the committee's tax adviser, joined them. The result of the auction depended on his assessment of Maher's ideas. Rosen was still thinking forty-five minutes later when Atkins interrupted him.

"What do you think?" he asked.

"I have some questions, but I think it'll work."

Peter Atkins trusted Rosen and told him to discuss his advice with the other lawyers and talk to Brian Finn in the morning.

At 4 A.M., Atkins and another adviser, Mike Mitchell, were the only ones left in the office. "I don't know what else we can do," Mitchell said. He stared at a copy of the First Boston letter on Atkins's desk. "How do you ignore something like that?"

Atkins nodded. He looked at Mitchell and sighed. "This is the way it'll have to be."

There were a few seconds of silence. The two men were old friends. Unless Rosen's talk with Finn changed the situation, they'd made their decision; all that was left was the special committee's approval Sunday morning.

"Whoever expected this to happen," Atkins said.

◆

Saturday morning, the special committee advisers talked with both Kravis's group and Cohen's group about their proposals and projections. Both explained the details of their bids.

Jim Maher walked around his apartment all morning, waiting for a call. He knew there was very little possibility First Boston's proposal would be accepted as a winning bid. At eleven o'clock, the call came. "Jimmy, you're going to get a letter," Atkins said.

A messenger delivered the letter five minutes later. The

questions were mostly tax questions. Atkins called several times that afternoon with further questions. Maher said he couldn't give definite answers without interviewing the RJR Nabisco executives. First Boston needed more information before it could guarantee the plan would work.

♦

Saturday evening, Ross Johnson had dinner with Jim and Linda Robinson at their Connecticut farm. All had heard rumors about the First Boston bid. They knew both the special committee and the entire board were meeting the following day. The committee would make a recommendation, and the board would probably agree with it.

During the meal, they called their friends to get more information. Finally, Johnson learned that planes for the directors' trips to New York had been cancelled. Apparently, the full board meeting had been cancelled.

"Why would they do that?" Johnson asked. "This is bad news for us." He paused and thought for a minute. "If the bids are close, we're dead. The board won't vote for us."

As they drove back to New York, Linda Robinson's car phone rang. It was a reporter with a press release that would soon be issued by the committee. She listened, not believing what she was hearing.

Then she called Johnson in his car. When he heard the news, he lost hope completely. "It's over," he quietly told his wife.

Johnson and the Robinsons joined the rest of the management group at Jack Nusbaum's office at Wilkie Farr & Gallagher. Everyone in the room was angry. Only Nusbaum felt positive. "We're obviously in a good position," he said. "The First Boston proposal won't work, and we'll still be the top bid."

"I don't believe it," Johnson said. "They know our maximum bid. The management group isn't going to get this bid."

Johnson was ready to quit and go home. "We always have the option not to bid again," he told the group. "Let's quit. Let them explain that to the shareholders."

For the first time, Peter Cohen began to realize that maybe Johnson wasn't an asset. Maybe the directors wouldn't give the company to him.

"Ross," John Gutfreund asked, "do you think this board is really against you?"

"They're not against me," Johnson explained. "They're for themselves. It's a big difference."

◆

By the time Hugel began the committee meeting Sunday morning at 10:15, everyone knew what had to be done. They couldn't ignore First Boston's proposal and its promise of a bid as high as $118 a share. In order to give Maher's group time to develop their plan, a second round of the auction would be declared. All bids, including the management group's winning $100 offer, would be thrown out. All would have to make new bids.

The directors agreed without much debate. The new deadline would be in ten days: Tuesday, November 29, at five o'clock.

◆

When he heard the news, Kravis didn't believe it. They should have lost. Johnson and Cohen had bid much higher. He hadn't imagined the management group would go as high as $100 a share. His anger turned to relief. "God," he said. "We have another chance."

That afternoon, when he and Roberts learned more details of the First Boston offer, they were shocked. They realized it was weak and couldn't believe the board had given Maher a second chance. But they were grateful.

Late that afternoon, Kravis, Roberts, and Beattie gathered in Kravis's office to plan their next bid. They agreed they were in a bad position.

"Wait," Roberts said. "We're in the exact position we want to be in." The others looked at him questioningly. "Let's just wait. We'll say we don't know what we're going to do. It's the truth. We don't have to say we're going to bid again. Let's let the world know we may not."

"You're right," Kravis said, understanding his plan. It made perfect sense: if they were going to make a strong bid this round, why let the others know? And if they didn't bid, they wouldn't be embarrassed.

Chapter 13   The Second Round

Monday morning, Jim Maher's team was excited. They'd succeeded when no one—not even themselves—had expected them to. Maher wasn't sure they could do this project. But they were going to try. They had only eight days to organize the biggest, most complicated takeover bid in Wall Street's history. This would be their test to succeed without Bruce Wasserstein.

Jay Pritzker flew from Chicago to meet with them. Maher explained the possibilities of RJR Nabisco. Mel Klein, Pritzker's assistant, wanted to meet with his friend Henry Kravis to discuss a possible partnership.

"We're not going to do anything you don't want us to do," Pritzker told Maher. "We just think we should talk with him."

Maher agreed. He'd be thrilled to split $25 billion with Kravis.

♦

Johnson was in a bad mood on Monday. "We weren't treated right," he told Hugel. "It's obvious to everybody."

"I really feel bad, Ross," Hugel said. "But there was nothing we could do about it. It had to be done this way. We couldn't turn down an offer that may be worth $110 a share."

Johnson still felt he'd been cheated by his own board, people he thought were his own friends. Steve Goldstone had been right. They weren't his friends any more. He hadn't wanted to believe it then, and he didn't want to believe it now. But Johnson knew it was true. He'd lost his own board's support.

There wasn't much his group could do to prepare for the second round. Johnson couldn't imagine going any higher than their $100-a-share bid.

"Whatever we do the second time," he told Jim Robinson, "it certainly can't be much higher than what we did the first time."

Wednesday afternoon, Johnson went to Florida for the Thanksgiving holiday.

◆

Everyone wanted to know what the other groups were doing. Dick Beattie talked with his friend Bob Millard at Shearson. "Congratulations," he said, "you guys sure had the best bid."

Then they discussed First Boston's surprise bid, and Millard wondered what Kravis might do next. Beattie said he didn't know. He sounded defeated.

It sounded like Kravis was out of the bidding. "Why don't you call Peter and congratulate him," Millard suggested. "I know he'd love to talk to you."

Beattie and Cohen talked that afternoon. "That bid was a winner, Peter," Beattie said. "Nice job."

"Thanks. What do you think of First Boston's proposal?"

"It's crazy," Beattie said. " It won't work. They can't do it."

"That's what we think, too," Cohen said. "We were really treated unfairly. What are you guys doing?"

"Oh, I don't know," Beattie said. "Everybody feels depressed. I don't know what we're going to do about this second round. We may not do anything."

♦

The board's advisers weren't enthusiastic about the entrance of a third bidder. The First Boston bid wasn't good news. They weren't confident Maher's group would have a strong proposal in eight days.

They were even more worried about Kravis's low bid. Was Kravis *trying* to lose? And their press release had suggested there might not be a second bid.

From the beginning, the committee's purpose had been to keep two strong bidders. When there were two, it aimed for more. It tried anything to produce the highest possible bid for shareholders. If both First Boston and Kravis failed to offer second bids, the committee was left with one alternative: Ross Johnson.

That made Felix Rohatyn, one of the advisers to the committee, uncomfortable. With two others, he formed two plans. First, Kravis had to be saved. They needed him to participate in the bidding next Tuesday. That meant giving him data and advice that showed RJR Nabisco was worth a strong second-round bid. Second, the committee had to make a new financial plan to use if Johnson was the only bidder.

The effort to save Kravis began Monday. "What do you guys need to get back in the bidding?" Lazard's Bob Lovejoy asked Paul Raether in a phone call that afternoon.

Raether said he needed more information if Kravis was going to think about bidding again. "We want to meet Ed Horrigan and the tobacco executives."

Raether had seen John Greeniaus's plan for saving money at Nabisco. He strongly suspected that Horrigan and Johnson had a secret plan for getting similar savings from the tobacco business.

"If there's a plan for that," Lovejoy said, "we don't know about it. They've said they don't have one."

Monday night, Lovejoy took a group to Kohlberg Kravis's offices to meet with Raether and Scott Stuart. They made a set of new projections for Kravis. They suggested an additional $150 million a year could be saved in the tobacco business. That was $8 or $9 a share, enough to increase Kravis's bid to over $100 a share.

♦

Tuesday, more than a dozen bankers and lawyers from Kohlberg Kravis and the special committee met with Horrigan at RJR Nabisco's New York offices. He was angry as he threw a newspaper article onto the table. That morning the *Greesboro* (North Carolina) *News & Record* was reporting that Horrigan and Johnson would be replaced if Kravis won the bidding. Even worse, the article was based on an interview with Paul Sticht, Horrigan's enemy.

"We don't know anything about that," Kravis said. "It's incorrect."

Horrigan talked about how Sticht had ruined the company and he'd rebuilt it. When he was through, Kravis's group began questioning him, but it was immediately apparent Horrigan wasn't going to help them.

"What can you do to cut costs?" they asked. "There have to be some savings here."

"No," Horrigan said, "there aren't. We don't waste money."

Horrigan's answers to other questions were the same. "There's nothing we can do. We can't do better."

"This is really fascinating," Kravis said after a while. "You can't do any better. And you can't cut anything. I think we overbid at $94. We made our first offer too high. I don't see how we can offer more."

Disgusted with Horrigan's performance, Kravis went to lunch with Jay Pritzker, Mel Klein, and Jerry Seslowe. He thought he might learn how seriously to take Maher's proposal.

Klein talked about RJR Nabisco and its cash flow and about First Boston's tax proposal and how they hoped it would work. The only way to improve their effort, he suggested, was if Jay Pritzker and his brother, Thomas, could team up with Henry Kravis.

"How would you like to work?" Kravis asked.

"We'll be partners," Klein said. "Fifty-fifty."

Kravis shook his head, no. "That's never going to happen. If we work together, you'll have less than 25 percent. You could make an investment with us. But we're going be in control."

"No," Pritzker said. "We don't have any interest in that."

It was obvious there wouldn't be a compromise.

That afternoon, the Kohlberg Kravis team separated for the holidays. Kravis went to Vail, Colorado, with his family.

◆

After spending Thanksgiving with his family, Jim Maher was back in his office on Friday morning. Tylee Wilson had joined his team. He was delighted to finally join the battle, although he had doubts about First Boston's chances of winning.

Maher was worried. None of their preparations would matter if the bank team couldn't obtain funding, and they were having trouble. Every major bank they'd asked had said no. Things didn't look good.

"*Maybe we ought to quit,*" Maher thought.

Then, Friday afternoon, Chase Manhattan agreed to look at their financing proposal. Maybe there was hope.

Maher's team worked through the weekend, moving slowly toward the Tuesday deadline. S & W Berisford, a British company Jay Pritzker owned stock in, agreed to contribute $125 million to finance the $1.2 billion in equity First Boston needed. In addition, the bank team had obtained multibillion-dollar promises from Credit Suisse and a French bank for the tobacco half of their plan.

That afternoon, however, they learned that Chase Manhattan wouldn't assist them. When Jim Maher heard the news, he closed his eyes. "*We're in big trouble,*" he thought.

◆

Friday night, John Greeniaus and his wife joined the Johnsons for dinner. Johnson talked about the wonderful opportunities Greeniaus would have after Nabisco was sold. "It'll give you and your guys a chance to be the top executives."

As the night went on, Johnson shared his concerns about the second-round bid. "One hundred dollars a share was a lot. I don't know if we can increase it," he said. "It was difficult the first time. Nothing's changed in the last ten days that would enable us to bid any more."

◆

Monday, *Time* magazine was in the stores. Ross Johnson's picture was on the cover with the headline: "A GAME OF GREED. This man could make $100 million from the largest corporate takeover in history. Have buyouts gone too far?"

Johnson's answers to questions for the story caused even more damage to his reputation. His response to a question about the possibility of many people losing their jobs was that in their professions—accountants, lawyers, secretaries—they could easily get other jobs. When asked about the management agreement, Johnson had said, "My job is to negotiate the best deal I can for my people."

◆

Monday morning, Felix Rohatyn met with the board advisers. There was a lot to do in the final thirty-six hours before bids were due. Everyone had heard the rumors about Kravis. And now they weren't sure about First Boston. They couldn't be certain that either group would bid on Tuesday.

Now, more than ever, they had to examine the possibility of restructuring. Luis Rinaldini, an adviser to the committee, had worked many hours on the plan and was sure it would work. Others had doubts. "What will happen to the company? Who will manage it?" they wanted to know.

The advisers decided to take a risk. They decided to tell bidders they wouldn't accept anything less than $100 a share.

◆

Tuesday morning, First Boston didn't know if they'd be able to bid. They still didn't have a bank helping them. Then, at noon, Harry Gray called Citibank again. They agreed to send a team to First Boston at two o'clock.

When they arrived, Fennebresque explained the situation. "In a few hours we have to put a bid in. One of the banks quit at the last minute. There's no doubt this bid is financeable. There *will* be bank money here. We'd like you to give us the most support you can."

For ninety minutes he explained First Boston's plan, and then he left them to prepare a letter.

At three o'clock, First Boston still needed $250 million. Mel Klein called a few investors he knew and managed to get several million dollars from each of them, but that wasn't enough.

Finally, he called Jay and Tom Pritzker.

"Jay, Tom," he said. "We're ready to go. We need a commitment for another $200 million. We don't have any other alternative."

There was a long silence. Mel Klein held his breath.

"OK. We'll do it."

Klein turned to Maher and gave him the news. For the first time that day, Maher had a reason to smile.

◆

At eleven o'clock Tuesday morning, Kravis and Roberts met with their investment bankers, telling them they hadn't decided whether they'd bid that afternoon. No one was concerned about First Boston. Kravis knew about Maher's increasing problems.

Afterward, Kravis, Roberts, and their group met in Kravis's office. Most, including Kravis, were ready to bid. No one in the room was surprised. They'd never believed he wouldn't bid on a deal this size.

"And if we bid," Kravis emphasized, "we bid to win."

Finally, George Roberts spoke, "I'm not comfortable with the idea we have to do this deal." Kravis and Roberts didn't often disagree. The others wondered what they'd do now.

"We started this firm on the basis that George and I are going to agree on everything," Kravis said, "or we're not going to do it at all." Roberts nodded.

"Wait a minute," said Jamie Greene, a San Francisco partner who was in charge of getting the billions of dollars in bank money Kohlberg Kravis would need if it bought RJR Nabisco. "George, I really think we ought to do this deal. Sure, it's going to be tough to do. But I think this is a wonderful deal."

"OK," Roberts said, "if we're going to do this, it's got to be safe. It's got to be a lot less cash than we've been talking about. The board's not going to be concerned with three or four more dollars in cash. They're going to look at the higher value."

For hours, they worked on their financial structure proposal.

At five o'clock, Kravis and Roberts returned to the boardroom with their announcement: a bid of $106.

◆

Peter Cohen and the management group met that afternoon at Shearson. Everyone had an idea what the bid should be. Some were suggesting $110 a share, but no one listened to them. Cohen and John Gutfreund had the only opinions that mattered.

Cohen favored a bid of $102 or $103. Gutfreund wanted to reduce the bid to $97 or $98. They compromised on $101, an increase of $1 from their last bid. They didn't need to bid higher because they didn't expect any competition.

♦

It was four thirty when the Citibank team leader gave their letter to Fennebresque. It was quickly put into the envelope, which was then sent to Skadden Arps. Their proposal wasn't what Maher had expected to produce, and their chances of success were small. But he'd won before—just nine days earlier.

"*Maybe it'll happen again*," he said to himself.

Chapter 14   The Winning Bid

Despite the *Time* magazine cover and the bad publicity that followed, despite the bad feelings among the board members, Cohen and Hill believed they were close to victory. No one thought much about Kravis. Everything now depended on First Boston. If the board believed Jim Maher's plan would work, First Boston would win. No one could compete with the returns Maher was promising.

When the management group hadn't heard from the special committee by nine o'clock, they started to feel nervous. The people waiting at Kohlberg Kravis were also anxious.

At nine o'clock, Dick Beattie took a call from Peter Atkins. "We'd like you and some of your team to come over here," Atkins said.

At Skadden Arps, they were met by Felix Rohatyn, Ira Harris, and Peter Atkins. Rohatyn explained that Lazard Dillon wanted to learn more about the securities Kravis proposed to include in his offer. Then he asked, "Is this your best offer?"

"Yes," Kravis said.

"Well, if we can get comfortable with the securities and financing, we're prepared to recommend your bid to the special committee."

Kravis and Roberts smiled. After six weeks, they were close to a victory. With luck, Kravis figured, negotiations could be finished in a few hours. The committee was scheduled to meet the next morning to make its recommendation. Kravis and Roberts could only wait.

After the meetings started, Atkins went upstairs to his office and called Jim Maher. First Boston's final bid had been quickly dismissed. The committee wasn't persuaded of Citibank's commitment to the project.

"I think you can go to sleep now," Atkins told Maher.

Linda Robinson was at a special dinner when she took a call. Angry, she immediately went over to Eric Gleacher, who had told her earlier that Kravis hadn't raised his bid. "Linda, you don't understand, do you?" Gleacher said. "There's no way this board's going to give this company to Ross Johnson."

Johnson, Horrigan, and the rest of the RJR Nabisco executives were waiting in their office when they heard the news. "That's it," Johnson said. "As far as I'm concerned, it's finished."

◆

As the evening went on, Goldstone walked around his office nervously. "*No news is bad news,*" he told himself. "*Maybe they're considering First Boston. Maybe, God forbid, Kravis's bid.*"

By nine thirty, he couldn't wait any longer and called Atkins.

"Are you guys going to make a decision tonight? Do we need to be waiting?"

"There's no reason for your people to wait around tonight," Atkins said. "We'll call you tomorrow."

"What does that mean?" Goldstone asked, his anxiety increasing. "Are we out of it?"

"I can't say any more. All I can tell you is, we don't need you tonight. You can tell your people to go home."

The management group was shocked. "*What does that mean? What's going on?*" they asked themselves.

Minutes later, they received a second shock. Nusbaum took a call from a reporter, who told him Kravis had just been called to Skadden Arps. "Has Shearson?" the reporter asked.

Nusbaum couldn't believe it. Peter Cohen couldn't believe it either. He knew something had gone terribly wrong. They had to do something fast.

Goldstone immediately called Atkins. "The management group has been cheated," he insisted. "We've been robbed of our victory by First Boston's crazy bid. As the first round's high bidder, we didn't have any reason to increase our offer. To be fair, there has to be another, final round of bidding. You have to keep the bidding open as long as people are willing to bid."

He continued for forty-five minutes. Atkins said he couldn't do anything until the committee met the next morning.

At eleven o'clock, Atkins received a letter written by Nusbaum stating that the management group had been at a disadvantage throughout the entire process. Nusbaum insisted the committee talk to them, since they were talking to other bidders. Other bidding groups had had an opportunity to bid against their first bid, so they should have the opportunity to respond to bids higher than theirs now.

Atkins frowned. It was going to be a long night.

At 11 P.M., Johnson called Hugel. "What's going on?" he asked.

"Kravis bid. A big one."

"How much?"

"I can't tell you." Talking to Johnson was against the rules of the auction process.

After a few more questions, Johnson figured it out. "You mean $106?" he asked.

"That's right."

Johnson was surprised. "OK. We're out of it," he said. "That's the end."

He returned to his group. "It's over," he told them. Because the bid was confidential information, he refused to answer their questions. He'd only say that Kravis's bid was much higher than theirs.

Then he called Cohen. "What do you mean they won?" Cohen asked. "Do we know what they bid? What happened?"

When Cohen insisted, Johnson said, "I can't tell you much. But I believe it's four or five dollars above ours. I can tell you, you're not going to beat a five-dollar difference."

At 12:30 A.M., Atkins called Goldstone. "I've discussed your opinions with our group," Atkins said. "All I can say is that your ideas of fairness in this auction process are incorrect. There was no unfairness. The auction won't be reopened."

"You have a legal obligation to hear us," Goldstone said calmly. "We want to bid again." Goldstone didn't know whether the management group wanted to bid again or not, but he wanted the option to be available.

Peter Cohen called everyone he knew to get information about Kravis's bid. He learned that Kravis had increased his bid by offering more securities than Shearson and less cash. "*If Kravis could do that, why couldn't Shearson?*" he thought.

He called Johnson. "We don't know enough to withdraw yet," he said. "We probably did lose, but let's wait until we know more about it. It looks like we could bid again."

"Well, what do you want to bid?" Johnson asked.

Cohen didn't know; he just wanted to keep his options open. Johnson couldn't understand how Shearson could possibly start the bidding again at this late hour. He certainly had no desire to.

Johnson called Goldstone. "Ross, it's their money," the lawyer said. "If they want to bid, you have to let them ... Unless you think you don't want to run the company, you have to let them bid. They have to bid something tonight. Tomorrow's too late."

Johnson thought the whole situation was crazy. At one thirty, Frank Benevento came in, excited. If the group increased the securities portion of their bid, they could increase its value without increasing its risk. Johnson wasn't sure. Hugel had always said cash was more important.

At 3 A.M., Johnson left and went to his apartment. He didn't want to be involved in the buyout any more.

Goldstone and Gutfreund, however, weren't ready to quit. If they wanted to win, they had to bid. And they had to bid right now. "Atkins isn't willing to reopen the auction," Goldstone told the others. "Decide your best bid and put it in now." He knew KKR would spend the night negotiating a merger. "You don't need to know the exact amount of Kravis's bid. Just bid."

By three o'clock, they were exhausted. By sunrise, Kravis would probably have a merger agreement. Gutfreund approached Cohen. "Peter, this was a great partnership," he said. "We worked well together, enjoyed it, and learned a lot."

"We'll win the next one," Cohen said.

◆

Negotiations at Skadden Arps went on through the night. Kravis, Roberts, and Raether waited in a conference room. Kravis was thrilled. The deal was almost over. As the hours went on, however, they wondered what was taking so long.

Then Bruce Wasserstein took a call from his partner, Joe

Perella, who was in Tokyo. Perella had just seen a story about the auction that would appear in the next morning's *Wall Street Journal*. It suggested Johnson might bid again. He sent a copy.

"What do you mean, they're going to bid again?" Kravis said. "The bids are closed!"

Roberts was angry. Someone, probably on the special committee, was leaking details of their bid. They probably wanted to get a higher bid from the management group. The Kravis group went to talk to the board's bankers, and a small group went into Atkins's office.

"Why are you talking to the management group?" one of the bankers asked. He was concerned about how angry Roberts was. "We're not supposed to be communicating with them. We're supposed to be doing a deal with KKR."

Atkins went downstairs to talk with Kravis and Roberts. Kravis was extremely angry. "We followed the rules," he said. He held out a copy of the *Journal* story. "Look at this. How did this happen?"

Atkins didn't say much.

Kravis and Roberts went to a conference room to make plans. The danger of a new Shearson attack was real. It was impossible to stop Cohen from bidding, but they could put a deadline on their bid to force the board to hurry and make a decision. They agreed on 1 P.M.—two hours after the board meeting the next morning. It gave the management group eight hours to attack.

◆

When Cohen woke the next morning, he called Tom Strauss. The Salomon executives were ready to fight.

Next he called Nusbaum at the lawyer's home. "What will stop us from making another bid?" Cohen asked.

"Nothing."

He told Nusbaum what he wanted to do.

93

Chapter 15   The Battle Ends

At 7:45 Wednesday morning, November 30, Atkins and the directors gathered in the Skadden Arps conference room. "We must try," he told them, "to reach a decision in the best interests of the shareholders. When anyone asks about what happened here, the response is 'No comment.'"

Then he told them about the previous night's events. "If Kohlberg Kravis's bid isn't accepted by one o'clock, they'll withdraw it," he concluded.

Felix Rohatyn noticed the directors' relief at being able to select Kravis as the winner. Ross Johnson had become a national symbol of greed. No one in this room wanted to give RJR Nabisco to him.

For three hours they discussed the bids. At eleven o'clock, Hugel told them Henry Kravis and George Roberts would be invited to address the board after a short break.

◆

Johnson felt much better that morning. It was good to have the whole fight over. At nine o'clock, Cohen called him in his office, excited. "We're going to make another bid. What do you think about going higher? The total amount's the same because we'll be using less cash. Will you agree?"

Johnson thought for a second. "OK," he said. This was Shearson's deal now.

◆

At 11:12, Kravis and Roberts walked into the board room, accompanied by Raether and Beattie. This was their chance to persuade the board that the Kohlberg Kravis bid was safe, secure, and in the best interests of employees and shareholders.

Roberts explained their plan. They wouldn't split RJR

Nabisco. They'd sell 20 percent of the company's assets, and shareholders would share in their profits. And they'd take good care of employees.

◆

At Shearson, Cohen's team had been busy all morning, and they finally had a bid ready. Now they needed Johnson's approval and his promise to further cut the management agreement if they won.

When Johnson heard Cohen's suggested bid, he laughed. He approved any changes to the management agreement that might be needed. Cohen returned to Nusbaum. "Put in this bid," he said. It was $108 a share. Twenty-five billion dollars.

At twelve o'clock, Cohen and Nusbaum had been waiting at Skadden Arps for an hour and had been ignored. They became anxious and decided they had to do something to reopen the bidding. "If they won't take the bid," Cohen told Nusbaum, "we'll announce it ourselves. Let's make a press release. The board can't ignore a public announcement."

When he heard about it, Atkins immediately went down to Nusbaum's office. Nusbaum gave him their bid. "Everything can be negotiated," he said.

Beattie was in the hallway looking for information. When he saw Atkins returning to the boardroom, he asked what Johnson and Nusbaum were doing. "We're going to have to consider what they've given us," Atkins responded. He wouldn't give any details.

"My guys are tired of this," Beattie said. "You have our best bid. We're going to quit if this takes too long. And if we quit, the other side can do whatever they want. You know that."

◆

Mel Klein was at the airport when he heard the bidding was open again. He was excited and called Jim Maher. After talking

95

for a few minutes about increasing their bid, they realized they were finished.

◆

Atkins returned to Kravis and Roberts at 12:40. "We've received something, and we need to extend your deadline."

They weren't happy about it, but they agreed.

At 12:50, a Kohlberg Kravis partner saw the headline RJR MANAGEMENT GROUP RAISES BID TO $108 A SHARE on the Dow Jones News Service. He immediately called Beattie.

Kravis sat down when he heard the news. It was twenty minutes before victory and everything had changed. The auction wasn't over. The company wasn't theirs. The world wasn't fair.

At one o'clock, Atkins called Nusbaum. He wanted to end the auction. "We want your highest and best bid," Atkins said. "We'd like it in fifteen minutes."

Nusbaum called Cohen and told him the bidding had been reopened. Cohen, who still didn't know Kravis's bid, called Goldstone. "We could go as high as $115," he told the lawyer. "I really think that's what we ought to do. It's time to end this."

Cohen explained that they needed Johnson to agree to cut the management group's fee from 6 percent to 4 percent. It was originally 8.5 percent. "Will you do it?" he asked.

"Sure, why not?" Johnson said, laughing.

Cohen called Nusbaum with his team's new bid. Nusbaum was surprised. He called Atkins with the news: Ross Johnson, Shearson Lehman, and Salomon Brothers were increasing their bid to $112 a share. At 1:24, Atkins delivered the news to the board.

The situation was suddenly complicated. One the one hand, Kravis had bid $106 a share, but his securities had been checked and negotiated. The bid's values were close to what Kravis had said they were. It was good. But it was second.

On the other hand, the management group had bid $112 a share, but their securities hadn't been checked and negotiated. There was no guarantee they'd trade at the prices Shearson said they would. Cohen valued his bid at $112, but it may have been worth only $105. The board needed time to determine its value. Atkins didn't have time. He needed to ask Kravis for another extension of his deadline.

The advisers had to find a way to keep Kravis from quitting. They didn't want to lose his bid. They decided to pay all his expenses—$400 million plus another $230 million if Johnson's group won.

Kravis met with his team. Instead of accepting Atkins's offer, they decided to increase their bid to $108, the same as Johnson's reported offer. "If both bids are the same," Kravis said, "we're going to win. Our proposal is better."

When they received Kravis's new bid, the board was surprised. They didn't know what to do. At 2:10, Atkins announced, "KKR just gave us its latest proposal: $80 a share in cash, $18 in stock, and $10 in securities."

"Any deadline?" someone asked.

Atkins thought for a moment. "No ..." Kravis had forgotten to set a new deadline. Now they had time.

First, they needed assurances that Cohen would agree to the same merger agreement Kravis had. He did.

Next, they had to determine the value of the management group's securities. Maybe they'd agree to use the same securities Kravis had used. They wouldn't.

It was obvious that every director in the room wanted to give the deal to Kravis. But since the management group's bid was higher, they had to check their securities. At 3:50, a team of investment bankers went to Johnson's offices.

The board discussed the situation for hours. At seven o'clock,

Johnson was tired of waiting and went out to dinner. Before leaving, he called John Martin. "What are our chances?" Martin wondered.

"They're not going to give it to us," Johnson said.

When he left the building, reporters shouted, "Who won? Who won?"

"The shareholders," Johnson said.

The board finally decided they had to give Kravis a chance to make a final bid, since they'd given Nusbaum a chance six hours earlier. Atkins and his group went to Kravis's office.

"If you haven't already done it," Atkins said, "this is the time to put in your best bid."

A half hour later, Beattie found Atkins leaning against a wall outside the boardroom. "Kohlberg Kravis has two requirements before it'll give you its final bid," he said. "First: A merger agreement must be prepared and given to the directors as part of the offer. Second, and most important, Kravis and Roberts want the board's promise that neither Johnson nor any member of the management group will be allowed into the final board meeting."

Atkins went to talk to Mike Mitchell and Dennis Block. They didn't know what to do, since Johnson was a chief executive of the company.

"You can't exclude him," Block said.

Atkins was getting desperate. The result of the entire $25 billion deal was at risk.

Suddenly, Mitchell asked, "Why don't we ask them if they plan to attend?"

Atkins called Goldstone and explained that the board was ready to meet and choose a winner. "Will your people be there?" he asked.

"Will KKR be at the meeting?" Goldstone asked.

"No."

"Then, no, we don't plan to be there unless KKR will be."

98

Atkins gave a sigh of relief.

He gave the news to Kravis, who then met with his team. "What should we bid?" he asked. The debate was tense. The result of the deal depended on their decision.

Finally, Jamie Greene said, "I don't know if we should change our bid or not. But if we do, let's increase it with a dollar in cash. We've come this far. We want to win this deal."

"I think he's right," Roberts said. "That's exactly what we should do. We want to own this company. Let's not ruin that chance now."

Kravis agreed. Greene's suggestion was quickly approved.

The last issue was a deadline. They'd forgotten it before, allowing the process to continue another six hours. They agreed on thirty minutes.

Beattie asked Atkins and Rohatyn to join them to hear their final bid.

Minutes later, Rohatyn addressed the board. Because Cohen and Gutfreund wouldn't allow their securities to be checked and negotiated, the management group's last bid couldn't be considered. "Therefore," Rohatyn explained, "the two bids are almost the same: $108 and $109. Both are fair from a financial point of view."

Now, the directors would have to make a decision. In their hearts, every person in the room knew how the board felt. The problem was finding a legal reason to feel that way.

Rohatyn explained the differences between the two bids. Finally, one director said, "Shearson's securities haven't been checked. That's not good enough. You don't do that in a $25 billion deal. We have to know what price those securities will trade at."

All nodded. Another mentioned Kravis's promises to treat employees more fairly. More nods.

Finally, they voted. All voted for KKR.

Atkins led a group of board advisers to Kravis and his group.

"Here's your signed contract," the lawyer said. "Congratulations. It's yours."

Then Atkins called Goldstone at the restaurant where he was eating. "I'm sorry to report the board has signed a merger agreement with KKR. The bids were close. But the board decided to sign with KKR for other reasons." He wouldn't give any more information.

Goldstone was silent.

Johnson took Goldstone's call at the restaurant where he was eating. "KKR got the bid," Goldstone said.

"Fine," Johnson said after a moment. "Let's get together and go see the guys."

In the RJR Nabisco office, Johnson talked with each of his executives and congratulated them for the good fight. Horrigan, however, complained. Despite Johnson's warnings, he'd never really believed they could lose.

When Horrigan blamed John Martin for the defeat, Johnson interrupted. "Gentlemen, we've been a great team. We've done a good job. If anything went wrong, it was my fault."

At midnight, everyone had left except Goldstone, the Robinsons, and the Johnsons. The five of them sat around the table.

"Do you remember that time we talked about the price of doing something like this?" Johnson asked the attorney.

Goldstone smiled. He thought about that day on the porch, long ago, it seemed, watching the red Florida sun go down.

Johnson laughed. "It surely was painful. Just like you said. But I'll tell you the same thing I told you then. I don't know what else I would've done. It was the best thing for the shareholders. It was the right thing to do."

Johnson's driver was standing, waiting. Johnson rose from the table and said, "Let's go home."

Business Wordlist

bankrupt   in a state of financial ruin

board   a group of people who manage, advise, or watch over a company

bond   a contract document promising to repay money borrowed by a company, often with interest

capital   money and property used to start a business or to produce more wealth

commerce   the activities involved in buying and selling things

corporate   relating to a large company, or corporation

currency   money, in coins and notes, which is used in a particular country

equity   the value of a property or of a company's shares; equities are shares that give you some of the profits

interest   payment received by a lender for the use of their money, or paid by a borrower

merge   to join together into one company

negotiate   to try to come to an agreement with another person through discussion

objective   a business aim

option   a contract giving a right to buy or sell at a particular price in a certain period

retail   the sale of goods to customers

return   the profit or income from an investment

security   something that you promise to give someone if you cannot repay money borrowed from them; securities are investments in stocks and shares

share   one of the equal parts into which ownership of a corporation is divided

speculate   to take a business risk in the hope of a gain

stock   investments in a company, represented by shares or fixed interest securities

underwrite   to accept financial responsibility for something

ACTIVITIES

Chapters 1–3

Before you read

1 Have you heard of RJR Nabisco? Which of its products are you familiar with?

2 Answer the questions. Find the words in *italics* in your dictionary. They are all used in this book.

   a When were you last *ambivalent* about something?

   b Have you ever been part of a *committee*? What were its responsibilities?

   c What are your *concerns* about your future at work?

   d Do you have an *extravagant* lifestyle? Describe it.

   e What *perks* would you like to have at work?

   f What significant *transactions* have you or your business made recently?

3 Find these words in your dictionary. Use them to complete the phrases.

   launch   quit   top

   a ..... your job

   b ..... a new product

   c ..... someone's offer

4 Read these sentences from the book. What are the phrases in *italics* in your language? Check in your dictionary.

   a In a *leveraged buyout* a small group of senior executives, with the help of a Wall Street partner, proposes to buy the company from the public shareholders.

   b "If you wish to proceed, the board will have to issue a *press release* tomorrow morning."

After you read

5 The following are important people in the story. Match the names with the statements about them. Which do you think are Johnson's friends? Which do you think are not?

   Peter Atkins   Jeff Beck   Peter Cohen
   Steve Goldstone   Ed Horrigan   Charlie Hugel

a Have you ever been to an *auction* of works of art? What happened?

b What *deadlines* do you have to meet at work at the moment?

c Are the *proceeds* of a sale your expenses or the money that you make?

d Why are sales *projections* helpful?

e Why might you worry if your company is *restructured*?

f What does a *round* of negotiations consist of?

After you read

17 Charlie Hugel thinks Johnson is lying to him. What do you think? Explain.

18 Complete the sentences.

    a Johnson says you can't put . . . . . first.

    b Greeniaus says Wall Street likes . . . . . .

Why do you think these statements are important?

19 Were you surprised by the bids? Why (not)?

Chapters 13–15

Before you read

20 Whose bid do you think will win?

21 What does the word *greed* mean, in the financial world?

After you read

22 Discuss these questions.

    a Were you surprised at the winning bid? Why (not)?

    b Have your feelings about Johnson changed? Why (not)?

Writing

23 Was Johnson concerned about his shareholders or only about himself? Give reasons for your opinion

24 One of Johnson's rules is that "The CEO can do whatever he wants." What do you think of this rule? Does it apply to companies in your country?

25 Which of the people in the book did you feel most sympathetic toward? Explain why.

26 Write a letter to Johnson, Kravis, or Forstmann. Make suggestions about what he could or should have done differently.

27 Johnson's reason for considering an LBO was that the company's share price was low. Explain why it was low. Were there any other ways of increasing its value, do you think?

28 Imagine what it is like being married to one of the top businessmen in the book. Write about the benefits and the disadvantages.

Answers for the Activities in this book are published in our free resource packs for teachers, the Penguin Readers Factsheets, or available on a separate sheet. Please write to your local Pearson Education office or to: Marketing Department, Penguin Longman Publishing, 5 Bentinck Street, London W1M 5RN.